THE DARK SIDE OXFORD

CRIME, POVERTY AND VIOLENCE

THE DARK SIDE OF OXFORD

CRIME, POVERTY AND VIOLENCE

MARILYN YURDAN

PEN & SWORD HISTORY

AN IMPRINT OF PEN & SWORD BOOKS LTD.
YORKSHIRE – PHILADELPHIA

First published in Great Britain in 2019 by
PEN AND SWORD HISTORY
An imprint of
Pen & Sword Books Ltd
Yorkshire – Philadelphia

ISBN 978 1 52673 965 0

Printed and bound in the UK by TJ International
Typeset in Times New Roman 11.5/14 by
Aura Technology and Software Services, India

Pen & Sword Books Limited incorporates the imprints of Atlas, Archaeology,
Aviation, Discovery, Family History, Fiction, History, Maritime, Military, Military
Classics, Politics, Select, Transport, True Crime, Air World, Frontline Publishing,
Leo Cooper, Remember When, Seaforth Publishing, The Praetorian Press,
Wharncliffe Local History, Wharncliffe Transport, Wharncliffe True Crime and
White Owl.

For a complete list of Pen & Sword titles please contact
PEN & SWORD BOOKS LIMITED
47 Church Street, Barnsley, South Yorkshire, S70 2AS, England
E-mail: enquiries@pen-and-sword.co.uk
Website: www.pen-and-sword.co.uk

Or

PEN AND SWORD BOOKS
1950 Lawrence Rd, Havertown, PA 19083, USA
E-mail: Uspen-and-sword@casematepublishers.com
Website: www.penandswordbooks.com

Contents

Introduction and Sources

The classic portrayal of Oxford is a beautiful, calm, healthy city. This has generated hundreds of works of over the years from poems of praise to tourist guides filled with beautifully tended gardens and manicured lawns, picturesque buildings, ancient traditions, shady walks and, of course, romantic trips on the river.

One of the chief instigators of this Oxford myth is Matthew Arnold's

'And that sweet City with her dreaming spires,

She needs not June for beauty's heightening'

from the poem *Thyrsis*, published in 1865, the year of the infamous Oxford bread riots.

Another is Gerard Manley Hopkins's

'Towery city and branchy between towers;

Cuckoo-echoing, bell-swarmèd, lark charmèd, rook racked, river-rounded'

from *Duns Scotus's Oxford* that appeared in 1879, for which *Jackson's* could quote the figures for pauperism for the city at 2.7 per cent of the residents, and the cost per head £6. 16s. 1¾d.

The great majority of books disregard the less attractive aspects of life in the city and the areas outside the influence of the university rarely even appear on maps designed for visitors. Until the mid-twentieth century outsiders had little reason to visit them, and if they did might feel somewhat ill at ease.

This book, on the other hand aims to represent accurately the lives of the ordinary citizens of Oxford, Town or Gown, from the Middle Ages to the end of Victoria's reign. This cut-off point was deliberate to avoid giving offence or causing embarrassment to close relatives of those who feature in the less pleasant incidents recorded. The contents are what the average citizen of Oxford is likely to have seen, heard or read. Some events were sensational but the great majority could have happened at any time.

Far from being special, apart from events directly related to the University of Oxford and its members, virtually any of the incidents included could have taken place in any other English city of comparable size and will show that at no time was Oxford an enchanted place, set apart from the rest of humanity.

It may be noticed that much of the activity took place to the west of the city centre in the extensive St Thomas's parish that included Jericho until St Paul's and then St Barnabas's parishes were carved out of it in 1836 and 1869 respectively. Also deprived was St Ebbe's where mean little terraced houses were crammed in rows on badly drained land. Many of these were owned by working class people who had struggled to purchase the properties and were hard pushed to maintain them properly. Although the whole town experienced loss at the Dissolution of the Monasteries in the 1530s, much of the inner areas were soon regenerated by the university taking over the sites of religious foundation and either converting them into new academic establishments or enlarging existing ones.

However, no later rebuilding in the western part of Oxford compensated for the loss of the extensive Grey Friars' site in St Ebbe's and above all of Osney Abbey, a great and well-respected foundation that counterbalanced the menacing Norman castle with its prison that continued to operate until 1996.

Until the nineteenth century, the Oxford darkness was, of course, literal and crimes are more easily committed under cover of darkness and more accidents take place in badly lit places. The first attempt at remedying this was oil lamps, followed by the 'Act for lighting with Gas the University and City of Oxford, and the Suburbs of the said City'. These suburbs would have been areas on the boundary of the city rather than the villages that later became drawn into it and were connected in 1869. The result was the Oxford Gas Light and Coke Company that dominated and disfigured St Ebbe's until 1960 when the works were closed, although two gasholders remained until their demolition in 1968. Gas street lighting was introduced in 1819. In 1882, with 3,690 customers on its books, the company purchased land on the south bank of the river and built new works and gasholders. Four years later, they built a railway to connect the works with the Great Western Railway network by a new bridge across the river.

In the 1880s a limited number of buildings had their own electricity generators. In 1890 the Electric Installation and Maintenance Company Limited of London obtained a licence and built a generating station at Osney and a distribution system for the newly formed Oxford Electric Company Limited. Their works opened in 1892 supplying electricity to only five street lamps and eleven businesses but three years later most of the colleges and some university buildings were being supplied.

Some of the dark themes cannot be adequately covered in this work and justify separate books. One that is mentioned at every court session is drunkenness: a vice, a cause of poverty and violence, an addictive illness, self-indulgence, a bad habit or simply a means of escape from the rigours of everyday life with the pub a sociable alternative to a cold and squalid home.

Other issues were begging and homelessness. However, although distressing for those involved and possibly frightening and even threatening for those approached, no attempts were made to find a permanent solution to the problem. In 1868 the Oxford Temperance, Prohibition and Band of Hope Association produced a facts and figures poster addressed to Oxford working men. It stated that £82,680 was spent each year at the city's 318 alcoholic drinks and tobacco outlets, of which 128 were ale and beer shops, 121 were hotels, inns and pubs, twenty-eight were wine and spirit merchants, twenty-six tobacconists with a gallon (4.5 litres) of ale or porter costing a mere two shillings, and fifteen brewers and maltsters. On the other hand, it argued that only £59,800 went on food at 230 traders in the city.

Another of the central themes of the book is death in all its many forms. In the November 1876 edition of the Quarterly Return of the Registrar-General of births and deaths for Oxford, including the Headington district, there were 184 deaths as opposed to 345 births and ninety-three marriages. The average number of deaths for the same quarter the previous three years was 230, composed of forty-eight infants under one year and fifty-two people aged 60 and over. The deaths included one from measles, two from scarlet fever, eight from fever, twenty-four from diarrhoea and ten from violence. There had been thirteen cases requiring inquests and nineteen deaths had taken place in public institutions.

INTRODUCTION AND SOURCES

Two aspects of life were unique to Oxford and Cambridge – the status of 'privileged persons' and the vice-chancellor's court. The *Chancellor and Proctors' Book* for 1290 gives a definition of privileged persons from that year. These were clerics and their families, college servants, bedels, parchment-makers, illuminators, writers, barbers and 'others who are occupied about the clothes of the Clerks etc., are to be held as included in the privilege of the University.'

This was a desirable status as records show severe punishment for those falsely claiming to have such positions. On 13 May 1447, two persons pretending to be scholars were found guilty of violence and, after a proclamation was issued, were banished from the town. A few weeks later on 28 June another pretender, Robert Shirleigh, met with the same treatment. However, belonging to university-related trades was no defence against insubordination. In 1446 a barber named William White and a bookbinder, Thomas Bokebynder, were imprisoned for speaking out against the proctors.

As the name suggests, a privileged person was one granted the privileges of the University of Oxford by being matriculated, that is by having his name entered onto the university roll. Most privileged persons were local tradesmen serving the university in the same way that the city fathers permitted only their own freemen to trade within its walls. Not surprisingly, this caused some dissatisfaction among local tradesmen and those who failed to live up to expectations might have these privileges withdrawn. It would be expected that privileged status would be discontinued after the Municipal Reform Act of 1835 but it went on until 1874. One of the main advantages was that privileged persons were available to represent the university during the long vacations when many of its members were away from Oxford, serving on juries, for example.

The vice-chancellor's court, formerly the chancellor's court, dates back to the earliest days of the university and is reserved for the use of its masters, scholars and privileged persons. Its jurisdiction was part religious, part secular, with much of it derived from royal charters. It dealt with the markets, rents, debt, keeping the peace and the upholding of morals and originally the proving of wills. The town was divided into six districts, each under the authority of a Doctor of Divinity and two Masters of Arts who dealt with complaints, or presentments. By the twentieth century actions were entirely civil, mainly cases of debt, and by mid-century it no longer had any practical use.

The university has long been represented as the cuckoo in the town's nest, and as an oppressor, but without its presence as upholder of the law and major employer over the centuries, it is likely that Oxford may have degenerated into just another market town and lost its status of county town as did Buckingham and Abingdon.

It would be possible to produce a companion book on improvements in Oxford over the years, but it would be nowhere near as interesting.

Sources

An appraisal of the following sources will give a more balanced view of the city and university as will any of the numerous memoirs and reminiscences that appeared in the nineteenth century.

The majority of references are taken from *Jackson's Oxford Journal*, abbreviated in the text to *Jackson's,* which first appeared on 5 May 1753. All references in the book are from *Jackson's* unless otherwise stated. The dates given for court cases are those on which the reports appeared in *Jackson's* rather than when the case was heard. An online version of *Jackson's* 1800-1900 can be accessed and searched through British Library Newspapers, and a printed synopsis of earlier editions can be found in the Westgate Library Oxford and the Oxfordshire History Centre.

Seventeenth-century material is mostly from Anthony Wood in *The Life and Times of Anthony Wood, Antiquary of Oxford, 1632-1695*, edited by Andrew Clark, Oxford Historical Society 1891-1900.

G.V. Cox, who lived and worked in Oxford all his life and became the university coroner, published his *Recollections of Oxford* in 1868.

Records generated by the vice-chancellor's court and the proctors are in the Oxford University Archives.

Most unusually, the Coroner's Roll of John of Osney 1297-1301, Oxfordshire History Centre, ref. P6/1L, is housed in the local record office rather than the National Archives.

Chapter 1

Antisocial Behaviour

The archdeacons' courts were nicknamed 'bawdy courts' because their best-known business was pronouncing on public morals and doling out penances mainly for fornication, and the vast majority of those censured were female. However, another offence for which parishioners might find themselves forced to perform acts of penance was for saying offensive things about their neighbours, and most of those involved men. These schedules started 'contrary to good Manners and Christian Charity'. One such penitent was John Hedges of St Clement's who, in March 1763, announced, in an audible voice, 'I have spoken and uttered certain Scandalous and Defamatory words of and against Hannah Cook of this Parish.' It is noticeable how many Oxford males were in trouble for defaming other men's wives. In 1770 William Uzzell of St Martin's parish had called Elizabeth Parker, wife of James Parker, 'a whore' and the following year John Bustin was in the same position for calling Jane Sims 'an old Bawd'.

This, however, was nothing compared with John Billingsgate's sentence for having a foul mouth which was to have his tongue cut out. This is how *Jackson's* recorded the event on 24 August 1753:

> 'He behav'd thro' the whole Affair with great Decency and did not swear above a Dozen Times from his House to the Foot of the Scaffold; when he came upon it, he told the Crowd he would make the last use of his Tongue in confessing the many Sins it had been guilty of. As he was beginning to rave, the Executioner told him his Time was elapsed and immediately performed his Business. Upon taking out the Tongue it blistered the hand that held it; and at several yards distance toasted Cheese like a Salamander. Great Quantities of Water were thrown upon it, but it was so much inflamed that it was found impossible to quench

it – Some Dogs that came within its Influence were seized with a sudden Fit of Barking and Snarling, but what was odd was, at the same Time they lost the power of Biting. The Tongue was at last purchased by a famous Logician who touches the Lips of those Pupils with it who want the genuine Spirit of Altercation.'

In February 1828 information was given by the constable of St Thomas's parish against a grocer and druggist named Faulkner, who had opened his shop for business on a Sunday morning. In his defence, Faulkner pleaded 'that the information was laid from a feeling of *revenge*, as he had complained of the *inactivity* of the constables of that turbulent parish, on a trial before the recorder (a man legally qualified to judge less complicated cases), a few days before; and stated that he believed himself to be the only person in that extensive neighbourhood whose shop was finally closed on a Sunday, at half-past ten o'clock, and that nearly every druggists' shop in Oxford was kept open throughout the day. Our worthy Mayor seemed to agree that the information was invidious, and dismissed the case accordingly.'

In 1835 university coroner G. V. Cox wrote:

'In this and several preceding years knocker-stealing appears to have been considered a manly feat by certain Undergraduates. Stealthily as those brave youths prowled about for their plunder, yet now and then a bungler in the operation was pounced upon by a Proctor or a policeman; and then ample remuneration was made at the expense of this individual, who had to pay a fine equal to the cost of the knockers wrenched off in the two or three preceding Terms!

'My fine old brass knocker in Merton Street was a special object of desire and attack. Several times, late in the evening, have I rescued it just in time, on hearing the grating sound of a bar or poker. Several times also, late in the night, I was disturbed by the well-known sound at my street-door, and on my shouting out "Police, Police!" away scampered the young peace-(if not house)-breakers. Christ Church fountain, on being cleaned out, soon after the cessation of this vile fashion, was found floored with knockers and broken fragments of sign-boards, ornaments, devices, &c.'

This, however, was not an end to the doorbell-ringing nuisance, for in June 1891 Louisa Dolling, a tobacconist of St Aldates, was summoned for disturbing John Hester by ringing his bell at quarter to three in the morning. She did not appear in court. Police Constable (PC) Goddard stated that he had seen her ringing the bell. Afterwards she went to the telephone office in Cornmarket and tried to ring the bell there, screaming 'Murder!' when he stopped her from doing so. Later she went to Hinksey where the constable was able to prevent her from going into the garden of a Mr Venables at which she promptly went round the side and rang the bell at the door there. The case was adjourned for a week, the bench being of the opinion that the woman should receive some kind of proper care.

In June 1849 George Carr was charged with annoying his neighbour and landlord, Thomas Clark, in Plantation Road. After he was given notice to quit, Carr lost no opportunity of annoying Clark by drawing sketches of coffins and gallows complete with a hanged man on Clark's door, as well as 'other subjects equally complimentary and agreeable to his feelings'. Unsurprisingly, this made Clark, who was of a nervous disposition, feel even more threatened and compelled him to involve the law. The defence stated that Carr was 'at liberty to indulge his taste for drawing on his own door' but the prosecution invoked a clause in a local act whereby when this was done to annoy another person it was punishable by a penalty not exceeding forty shillings. In addition Carr had used abusive language likely to cause a breach of the peace towards his landlord and offered four witnesses. The magistrates suggested that Carr should apologize, promise not to reoffend and leave the house within a fortnight. This he agreed to do and was discharged after paying six shillings for expenses.

A cautionary letter appeared in *Jackson's* of 21 June 1851, warning the charitable to beware of being tricked into parting with their money to undeserving causes. J.C.T. writes: 'Yesterday a woman named Rixon applied to me for assistance to enable her to buy some leeches for her child, two years old, who had a turn [appointment] given to her for the Dispensary, stating that every thing but leeches was provided by Mr. Wood,' naming a local surgeon. The writer had contacted this medical man and of course he knew nothing about it. He had been the subject of similar applications previously but after he started to make enquiries these had all but stopped and so he was writing to advise anyone else in this position to do the same.

In November 1855 Fanny Crapper, an inmate of the penitentiary in Brewer Street, was charged with breaking windows and behaving riotously at that establishment. On promising to behave better in future she was allowed to return to the penitentiary.

In January 1867 Thomas Faulkner, a shoemaker aged 32, pleaded guilty to wilful damage to plate glass worth seven pounds in a window belonging to James Sheard. The recorder stated that if the offence had been committed after nine o'clock in the evening Faulkner would have been liable to transportation; as it was, he received four months' imprisonment.

Lord Randolph Churchill of Merton College was summoned before the vice-chancellor and the President of St John's College on two charges in March 1870. One was for assaulting PC Partridge while he was going about his duty and the other of being drunk and riotous ten days previously. The Police Committee of the city corporation prosecuted and Churchill conducted his own defence 'in a manner that would reflect credit on many a Barrister.' Heavy charges were not thought necessary for the first offence merely to show that the 'police could not be assaulted with impunity.' It was clear 'that the policeman in the case was hustled in a foolish freak, and his helmet taken away', which constituted a breach of the peace. PC Partridge described how he had been in Beaumont Street just after midnight when the defendant came out of the Randolph Hotel. He took hold of the constable, pushing and shoving him before taking hold of his cape. At least a dozen more students followed Partridge, grabbed him and knocked off his helmet. Churchill offered him five shillings for it but was refused. He then ran along Magdalen Street into Cornmarket, followed by about twelve others. PC Partridge followed and overtaking Churchill asked for his name and address, which he refused to give. Partridge threatened him with the police station, and Churchill said he would like to go as he had never been there. On arrival he gave his name to the duty inspector. Statements were taken from several witnesses, both police and students, and it was disputed that it was in fact Churchill who had knocked off the helmet and Partridge admitted that he could not swear to this.

The Christ Church outrage or 'university rattening' made the national newspapers in May 1870. A group of young men carried busts and statues, some of them very valuable, out of the college library at Christ Church and positioned them round Peckwater Quadrangle. What followed provoked general horror and disgust nationwide. A second group came along, gathered up material to make a bonfire and threw the statues on it. Unsurprisingly, they were far gone in drink, but this was no excuse whatsoever, even allowing for the so-called high spirits of youth. The *Jackson's* reporter comments that many of these young men would have had, at times, 'no more consciousness of right and wrong than the unfortunate inmates of a lunatic asylum'. By contrast, continues the reporter, even the humblest of the countrymen of these members of the university would treat national art treasures 'with such scrupulous care that it would seem as if each man felt himself to be their conservator.' Conversely, those who came from some of the best families in the country, and should have known better through both their birth and education, had refused to own up like men and their companions had not 'sought to purge the university of its foul stain by bringing the guilty to justice' through a misplaced sense of loyalty. A meeting was held in college passing a resolution that the outrage was regarded with the utmost regret but no indication that this was strong enough to tell tales.

A few days before St Giles's Fair of 1876, the mayor had issued a notice to the effect that because there had been numerous complaints to the justices of the peace about the 'squirts, scratch-my-backs and other instruments of personal annoyance', a special meeting was held. It was decided unanimously to put a stop to these nuisances by making this an assault, the punishment for which would be a fine not exceeding five pounds or a prison sentence of two months. The police were directed to arrest all offenders but to make doubly sure supplies of the offending items were cut off, another notice was posted that any person found trying to sell any squirts, scratch-my-backs or crackers would forfeit their pitching money and be prevented from selling any other goods at the fair. These measures, said *Jackson's*, had the desired effect. However, the following year, a substitute had been found in short India-rubber whips, which were used occasionally 'with "striking", but probably unintentional vigour'. And in 1879, even though the offending items from previous years were absent, a worse nuisance appeared in the form of handfuls of flour, bran and sawdust thrown deliberately into the faces of people strolling round the fair. Rice was also being thrown although this was not found as objectionable as the other 'tormentors'. In 1880, previous annoyances having disappeared, 'the youthful mind was somewhat at a loss to devise some form of amusement, and ultimately it took the form of bunches of dried grass, long feathers etc, which were put in people's faces. But this harmless fun was found to be too tame for some of the more mischievously inclined and cayenne pepper was dusted in the faces of several persons whose eyes suffered severely in consequence.' On 10 September 1892 William Jones, a tramp of no fixed address, was charged with being drunk and disorderly in St Giles at quarter past eight on the Monday evening of the fair. Jones pleaded guilty and PC Harris stated that the prisoner was singing in the fair and annoying people by pushing a handful of song books in their faces. When he was spoken to he used filthy and abusive language and was sentenced to seven days' hard labour.

In December 1881, Emily Sleath, landlady of the City Arms, was summoned by the School Board for employing a girl named Hannah Parker as a servant, at an age at which she should have been at school. She pleaded guilty and said that she hired the girl through ignorance of the law. The attendance officer told the bench that there were a good many instances of children being employed under age. The bench stated that the child must attend school, and the defendant would be fined half a crown and six shillings costs.

William Holt of Albion Place, St Clement's, was charged in August 1882 with being drunk and riotous and using obscene language. Holt, 'a well-known noisy hawker of newspapers' admitted that he had been into several public houses but denied being drunk. PC Butler said that Holt had been very drunk and was making use of coarse and obscene language. He was very noisy and drew a large crowd round him. In the dock the prisoner behaved 'in a wild and strange manner' insisting that he was called Matchy's murderer, which he was not, and Solomon, who he also was not, for he had not 300 wives and 700 concubines, which caused laughter in the courtroom. If the policeman swore that he was drunk, he went on, he must bow to his decision, and await the wrath of the Lord. Mr G. Ward said that he thought the prisoner was not in his right mind. Holt retorted that our Lord and St Peter were not in their right minds when they were before their judges, and he wished they would ask William Ewart Gladstone if he was mad. More laughter. The bench thought the charge proved, and inflicted a fine of six shillings and four shillings and sixpence costs, or seven days' hard labour and Holt was warned that if he appeared again for a similar offence he would receive a much more severe sentence.

Edward Hilsdon, a labourer from Magdalen Road, was summoned in February 1886 'for throwing a missile, namely a snow-ball' some three weeks previously. PC Mott said that Hilsdon had been clearing the street of snow to take away to Port Meadow in a cart near the Clarendon Press in Walton Street. He picked up some snow from the cart and threw snowballs at several people, including three young girls who were on their way to the University Press. When the constable reprimanded Hilsdon, he said that he had done it for fun. PC Mott's evidence was corroborated by a painter named James Edgington of Worcester Terrace. Hilsdon was fined one shilling and four shillings reduced costs.

In May 1886 shoemaker Charles Cudd of Cranham Street, Jericho was charged with deliberately breaking six panes of glass valued at thirty-five shillings at the Harcourt Arms in Cranham Street. He pleaded guilty and added that he had told the landlord, Frank Kemp, that he was going to do it. Kemp stated that he had wished the prisoner good morning at seven o'clock only to be greeted with some very offensive language and shortly afterwards Cudd had broken all of the pub windows for no reason that Kemp could think of. Cudd claimed that Kemp had assaulted his wife, but this the landlord completely denied and said that the prisoner was in the habit of accusing people of interfering with 64-year-old Mrs Cudd. The Cudds' daughter told the court that her father 'had a fancy that his wife was unfaithful to him, but there was no reason for it.' The bench decided that there was no excuse for such behaviour or making these accusations and he would be fined five shillings with four shillings and sixpence costs and have to pay the cost of repairing the windows or go to prison for a month. Cudd commented 'I must go to "college" then.'

On 10 July 1886, William Allen of Fisher Row was summoned for stone-throwing with a catapult in Bridge Street, Osney. He pleaded guilty and PC Prior stated that on passing along the street he found Allen being held by Mr Lewis in his house because he had slung a stone through his window with a catapult. He had found a stone in the room and picked up several pieces of broken glass near to where the Lewis family had been sitting. He found several stones in Allen's pocket. The damage done amounted to one shilling and sixpence. The magistrates said that this was a dangerous practice which they would do their best to stop and Allen was fined half a crown with six shillings costs.

Hannah Simmons of St Thomas's was summoned in June 1888 for damaging grass belonging to Albert Cook of the Old Gate House, growing in a field in Binsey Lane. She pleaded guilty and PC Hawes stated that he found Simmons with another woman and two men rolling in the grass and having a bottle of beer with them. They were fined five shillings with six shillings costs and three-pence damage, or seven days' imprisonment.

At the city police court a casual inmate of the workhouse named William Reynolds appeared in May 1894, charged with refusing to do the work allocated to him. On his first morning at the institution, Reynolds had been presented with three hundredweight of stones to break. William Carter, the deputy relieving officer, told the court that the prisoner had refused point blank to do this. When examined, Reynolds told the court that the workhouse authorities had removed his food. It was decided that he should be imprisoned for a week.

On 8 May 1894, Richard Chesterman, a labourer living in Friars Wharf, stood accused of being drunk and disorderly in Queen Street at ten past eleven the same morning 'holloaing and waving his arms in the air.' Chesterman stated that he was very sorry for the way that he had behaved and was sentenced to a day in gaol. At the same court, Richard James Manion from Jericho was summoned for causing an obstruction in Jericho Street by leaving his butcher's cart there overnight.

Private soldiers James Williams and George Martin were charged in April 1899 with being drunk and disorderly in Blue Boar Street at midnight. Williams was also charged with being a deserter from the Oxfordshire Light Infantry (OLI) stationed at Cowley Barracks, and Martin with being a deserter from the Berkshire Regiment, stationed at Reading. Both prisoners pleaded guilty. However, Stephen Hammock, an officer with the OLI said that Williams had been present at the barracks on the Monday and so could not therefore be a deserter. Police Sergeant (PS) Furmage said that the prisoners had come to the police station drunk and asked for tickets for the workhouse. Williams was fined a shilling with three shillings and sixpence for being drunk and Martin was remanded to await an escort back to Reading.

On 2 September 1899 groom William Ellis and unemployed Albert Morris, both of Divinity Road, were summoned for being drunk in Oxford High Street one Saturday afternoon. PC Baker stated that he saw them there, carrying guns. They were annoying passers-by and aiming the guns at windows. They were very drunk and when he got them to the police station he searched them. The guns were not loaded and they had no cartridges on their persons. PS May and a farmer named Blay also gave evidence and the defendants were fined a pound with seven shillings and three-pence costs or one calendar month's imprisonment.

Chapter 2

Assaults

The records generated by the eyre, or travelling court, throw a considerable amount of light on the violence of life in the Middle Ages. The following are examples from ones that sat in Oxford. A comprehensive array of weapons is mentioned in Latin and it should be remembered that every citizen, man, woman and child, carried a knife with which to cut up their food. An even more disturbing aspect of this violence is that the villains and victims, if members of the university, would have only been in their early to mid-teens, a tragic waste of promising young lives.

David fitzGriffin laid a complaint against Richard de Tangele, Valentine his brother, and John de la Rede, on the grounds that, on 29 May 1284, David was quietly minding his own business outside the North Gate, on his way to his lodgings just as it was getting dark when he came across a certain chaplain carrying the Host to some sick persons. As David genuflected to pray before the body of the Lord, Richard and Valentine assaulted him. Richard struck him with a sword on his left shoulder, giving him a wound six inches long, so that David was in despair of his life. Afterwards, Valentine and John beat him almost to death with their swords to his serious damage and contrary to the King's peace. He experienced suffering and damage to the value of £133 6s 8d, and for that reason he brought the action.

On 18 January 1296 an inquest was held before the town coroner and two bailiffs concerning a burglary at St Frideswide's church involving a disturbance of the peace and an assault made in Catte Street. The sworn jury including men from the parishes of St Mary the Virgin and St Cross, related how Robert, Henry, Simon and Hugh de Spalding were present when the church was burgled and that they were notorious robbers and 'night-wanderers'. They added that these men, along with Adam de Wolneeby, and his friend Stephen, both residing in Hare Hall in Kybold Street, and Hugh Pychard, living in the house of John de Ducklington near the East Gate, came to Catte Street late in the day, and with drawn swords and knives attacked anyone who crossed their path. They beat and wounded them and treated them very badly, one of their victims being a woman named Emma le Wilde whom they hit across the back with a sword so that it was doubted that she would live.

An inquest was held at Oxford on 20 August 1389 before two aldermen, one of the king's coroners, two bailiffs and two of the town's constables. The sworn jury stated that John Coughwel of Watlington made an assault on Thomas Hosebonde, an Oxford fuller, with a two-handed sword, on the East [later Magdalen] Bridge. He beat, wounded, ill-treated him and maimed him by breaking his arm in two places so that it was thought that he would not survive. The jury also said that the accused assaulted John Mason of Cornwall, and almost cut off one of his arms with his sword. He also went to All Saints parish one night and set upon a tailor named Welshman, beat him up and nearly cut off his thumb with his sword. In addition, he assaulted Hugh Hedeworthe, breaking the King's peace and terrorizing the neighbourhood. He also attacked one of the bailiffs' men who was going about his business, made an assault in All Saints with a long dagger and, when John Forester, one of the bailiffs saw him committing these offences and disturbances and tried to arrest him, he resisted arrest, taking him by the neck and held him by force so that he drew blood. He openly threatened many townspeople, saying that he would beat and kill them when he got the chance. The jury concluded that he was a common disturber of the peace as well as a brawler and troublemaker.

On oath, the jury swore on 13 September 1389 that on 29 August, William, manciple (the person in charge of buying in provisions) of Paul Hall on the north side of Pembroke Street, William Alkebarwe, John Grisell, Roger Weyt, Henry Benton, Adam Perle and others broke the windows of the Grandpont house of Richard Bowyer. Armed with axes and other tools, they intended to make their way into the house, using the password 'chop-cherry', kill him and steal his belongings. The jury also said that on the same day, William and the others robbed Robert Mayde, manciple of St Laurence Hall in All Saints parish of a torch worth four shillings and beat and wounded him so badly that his life was despaired of. They also said that William allowed into his house in St Ebbe's parish a certain Robert Skinner from London with a ruby-coloured tunic worth eight shillings, another russet one worth five shillings and a fur worth sixteen shillings, knowing that Skinner had stolen them from Elizabeth Woluesham of Botley and knowing that he was guilty of the murder of a woman in Cock Lane, London.

The records of the chancellor's court also illustrate how the university attempted to deal with aggressive behaviour. On 28 June 1447, William Carpenter, a townsman, was banished from Oxford for shooting at the proctors. Three years later John Martyn, a schoolmaster from the parish of St Michael at the North Gate, who was already under threat of excommunication, conspired with his scholars that as his sentence was being read out, they should snatch the document from the priest's hands and drag him out of the pulpit. Martyn was imprisoned along with the ringleaders among his pupils.

On 27 June 1452 a Master Richard Denoyty was charged with having carried weapons and got together a gang of armed louts intent on disturbing the peace.

Having knifed a man, John Harry, a tailor described as a 'scissor', fled for sanctuary to Broadgates Hall, now part of Pembroke College, on 25 August 1453. He was chased by the proctor and, despite his protestations of innocence, was dragged out of the building and taken into custody, with a promise that he might be allowed back into sanctuary should his life prove to be in danger. In the event, it turned out that the knife wound was not as bad as had been feared and a fellow tailor was allowed to stand bail for Harry on the usual terms. The accused then had to appear in court to answer the charge.

Anthony Wood, too, follows the violent behaviour of his age. John Bradshaw from Kent, a scholar at Corpus Christi College broke into a little garret on 13 July 1677 and then into the chamber of college Fellow, John Weeks, who had gone to bed. Bradshaw stole twenty-five shillings and proceeded to hit Mr Weeks on the head with a hammer, but the head of the hammer came off and did no harm.

On 29 September 1684 a notice was posted in a public place within the university area to the effect that John Osmond, a debauched Master of Arts of New Inn, had been expelled for biting off a piece of the nose of Thomas Greaves, Bachelor of Arts, of Brasenose College in the course of a scuffle which had taken place in the University Parks a few days previously.

At an assault case heard in the vice-chancellor's court and reported in *Jackson's* on 19 November 1883, the court was told how the Honourable

Charles H.F.S. Trefusis of Christ Church and David Guthrie of New Inn Hall had assaulted PC Beckwith. Guthrie was also charged with deliberately smashing a pane of glass at the police station. PC Beckwith related how several undergraduates had crossed the road and had met him. One of them had said, 'Well, Bobby, have you got any more reports for the Proctors against us?' This referred to the previous week when he had reported an offence to the proctors, who had dealt with it strictly. One of the students said, 'Let him have it', and part of a pineapple was thrown at the policeman, hitting him in the face. He took hold of Guthrie and with the help of a colleague was taking him off to the police station when Trefusis also hit him across the face. Both students were taken to the police station where, when he caught sight of a constable looking through a glass door, Guthrie thrust his hand through it, saying, 'That is for you.' The defendants pleaded guilty and were fined ten pounds each and made to pay costs and damages.

Every edition of *Jackson's* carries examples of assaults with an account of how the law dealt with them, some of the outcomes being rather unexpected.

From 28 July 1849 at the city court: 'Abraham Davis, a Jew, made a complaint against Louis Solomon, of the same persuasion, for assaulting him by knocking him about with the candlesticks in the synagogue in Paradise Square' the previous Sunday. An argument had arisen between them in the synagogue regarding some expenses and angry words that quickly turned to blows were exchanged. Candlesticks and stools belonging to the synagogue were damaged. The magistrates advised the pair to make up their quarrel but Davis was unwilling to start with and 'seemed resolved to let the public into the mysteries of the synagogue, and the disorderly brethren who were there on Sunday last.' Ultimately the advice was taken and the pair left the court.

From 4 October 1851: Ellen Ludlow, a single woman, appeared before the city court with a face covered in scratches 'evidently the result of a collision with one of her own sex' to make a complaint against Sarah Butler, the wife of Joseph Butler, for a violent assault at a lodging house in Orpwood's Row, St Thomas's. The defendant brought a counter-charge for striking her on the mouth with a poker which had prevented her from eating ever since. In order to understand better who was at fault, the case was adjourned for three days.

At the same sitting, Mary Anne Dorrell was charged with having violently assaulted Mr Clempson in St Thomas's 'and giving him the benefit of a serious black eye.' Dorrell pleaded guilty but explained that she had been celebrating the return of a friend 'who had been shut out of society for a twelvemonth by being locked up in gaol, and that having taken seven glasses of rum to commemorate so auspicious an event, she was not aware who she had assaulted, or whose eye she had damaged. [Dorrell] having begged pardon for the mischief she had done, and promised to be a very reformed character for the future, the complainant kindly agreed not to press for a fine, and the defendant was accordingly discharged on promising to pay the costs, amounting to 5s, within a certain time.'

On 21 August 1852 appeared a report of an intriguing affair. At the city court Eliza Fathers, Emma Wilsden and Harriet Nethercote were charged with a gross and indecent assault on Sarah Butler of Jericho. Fathers and Wilsden were convicted and fined five pounds each or be imprisoned and kept at hard labour for two calendar months. Nethercote was acquitted and discharged.

From 18 December 1852: Charles Gilliam, a chair-maker, was convicted of assaulting William Williams, one of the university police, and rescuing a prostitute named Sarah Brown from his custody, as he was taking her to the university police station. The defendant was fined twenty shillings, and costs of seven shillings and sixpence, and in default of payment he was committed to gaol for twenty-one days with hard labour.

From 4 July 1857: Thomas Chesterman, aged 20, was charged with assaulting William North, a university policeman while he was on duty in St Thomas's. He heard the prisoner and a woman creating a disturbance in the street and advised them to go home quietly, which they appeared to do. Shortly afterwards, however, he heard cries of 'Murder!' coming from a house in Lamb and Flag Yard where he saw the prisoner with tongs in his hand about to strike the woman, who was already covered with blood. North rushed to her aid and parried the blow with his staff. Chesterman, who was drunk, then ordered him out of the house, waved his fists in his face and threatened to kick him out. However, no blow was in fact struck and North left the house.

The defence made a clever contention; had the charge been that of assaulting the woman it would have been valid, whereas the prisoner had not touched the policeman merely ordered him out of the house where he had no right to be as he had not been sent for. The recorder told the jury that the act of holding up one's fists within striking distance of another person did constitute an assault. After a brief deliberation, the jury returned a verdict of not guilty. Chesterman was discharged with a caution to be more careful in the future.

From 23 July 1870: Josiah Page of the Coach and Horses Yard, High Street, was charged with assaulting Ann Surman. She complained that she had quarrelled with Page's wife because she had thrown dirty water over her and when Page had returned home he had thumped her round the face and head. Page admitted the punches but pleaded great provocation, and because of an attack of rheumatic fever he had become very excited and could not always control his temper. The mayor told Page that he was a dangerous character and would have to avoid excitement. Page paid the five shillings fine and seven shillings and sixpence costs rather than seven days' hard labour.

From 11 September 1875: Elizabeth Goodenough alias Ann Elizabeth Beesley, alias Ann Walton, of Red Lion Square, pleaded guilty to assaulting Charles Thatcher, ostler at the Roebuck Hotel. There was a cross-summons between the parties, and Elizabeth Drinkwater, Cardigan Street, also pleaded guilty to assaulting Beesley at Thatcher's instigation. The bench thought that Thatcher had ruined the woman Beesley and then turned her off, and his conduct had been disgraceful in the extreme. He would have to undergo two months' hard labour and be bound over to keep the peace for six months and Drinkwater was given twenty-one days' hard labour. Thatcher was removed exclaiming that he was ruined for life.

From 27 September 1879: under the heading 'Life in St Ebbe's' *Jackson's* reported on a charge of assault by Sarah Abel of New Street, St Ebbe's on a neighbour, Elizabeth Penn, aged 33. Penn claimed that Abel had pushed her off the pavement and called her a 'nasty, stinking, lazy old cat'. She had been similarly annoyed before. Abel said that Penn 'had set up a horrid laugh' against her, and called her a stinking old cat on a different occasion but Penn denied both of these accusations. Abel admitted to calling Penn a 'lazy good-for-nothing wretch' and that she had pushed her off the pavement because she could not pass. She was fined one shilling and seven shillings costs, or seven days' imprisonment.

From 27 September 1879: William Udell, Chapel Terrace, St Clement's was charged with using threatening behaviour towards Caroline Rumball of Chapel Terrace. The court heard that the prisoner told her that 'if she put him to more expense he would put a bullet through her and tear her heart out.' This sort of behaviour had been going on for months and she was afraid of him. She had four children by Udell and all she wanted was to have him bound over not to molest her again and she would provide for the children as best she could. Udell was bound over in twenty pounds to keep the peace for twelve months.

From 30 July 1892: Eliza Cunningham, flower seller of Eagle and Child Yard, St Giles, was charged with assaulting Henry Denny in High Street, St Thomas's, by striking him on the forehead with a pair of scissors with intent to do him bodily harm. The complainant, who lived in Hollybush Row, St Thomas's, said that he had seen Cunningham with her husband John who struck him under the eye with his fist. The blow knocked him over and he fell into the doorway. The woman then 'jobbed' a large pair of scissors into his forehead. He struggled to get up, only to be knocked down again and the scissors plunged into his head three or four times. Passers-by pulled the couple away and a gentleman took Denny to the Radcliffe Infirmary. The bad feeling had been caused by Denny and his wife's refusal to drink with or speak to the Cunninghams. John Cunningham was present in court and made to stand next to his wife. Denny denied striking either of the Cunninghams and witness Henry Dry corroborated with the Dennys' evidence and added that he had told the woman that she ought to be ashamed of herself to which she replied that she did it because 'he struck her cowardly that morning.' Another added that Denny had not struck the Cunninghams at all. They finally pleaded guilty and were sentenced to two months' hard labour each, and to be bound over in the sum of five shillings to keep the peace for six months, or twenty-one days' hard labour more.

From 25 March 1893: James W. Gandy, an auctioneer's assistant of no fixed address, was charged with being drunk and disorderly at the Great Western Railway Station at quarter to six one Monday afternoon. He was also charged with assaulting PC Day in the execution of his duty and biting him on the arm and assaulting train driver, Sidney Gibbs on the same occasion. He pleaded guilty. PC Day said that he was called to the prisoner who was drunk and kicked, hit and bit him. Gibbs said that Gandy had tried to get out of a moving train and Gibbs was forced to stop it as the prisoner was 'mad drunk'. Gandy said that he was very sorry for what he had done and promised never to do it again. He had never behaved like that before. It was queried why he had been allowed on the train in such a state in the first place to which Mr Davis, the station master replied that Gandy had got on at Birmingham and had not been like it there. It seemed that he had left the train and bought alcohol at several stations en route. He was fined half a crown with three shillings and sixpence costs for being drunk, five shillings and three shillings and sixpence costs for the assault on the police officer, or seven days' imprisonment for each offence; 'the assault on Gibbs to stand over' to be tried later.

Chapter 3

Domestics

Unfortunately, differences between husbands and wives came to blows only too frequently in certain parishes.

An inquest was held in May 1842 on the body of Thomas Milsham, publican of the parish of St Clement's, aged 34 who had been committed for an assault on his wife, and died in the gaol the same morning. George Bossom, keeper of the gaol, deposed that Milsham had been fined five pounds for the attack, and in default of payment was to be imprisoned for two months. When brought into the gaol he appeared to be stupid with drink, with blood all over his clothing. Because of all the noise that Milsham was making, the surgeon to the gaol, Mr Rusher, was sent for to examine the prisoner's hand which he had cut on some glass. He ordered that Milsham be taken from his cell to the kitchen to be quiet and he was locked in alone. He said nothing to the surgeon about how he came to end up in gaol.

Between seven and eight in the evening, Rusher found it necessary to put the prisoner into a 'straight-waistcoat' for his own protection and it remained on him until the next morning. Rusher considered that Milsham was not in his right mind and he died that morning about eleven-thirty. The jury returned a verdict 'died from *delirium tremens* brought on by excessive drinking.'

In July 1875 James Knibbs a labourer aged 45, was indicted for unlawfully assaulting, beating, wounding and ill-treating his wife, Eve, at Oxford, thereby occasioning actual bodily harm, on 16 June the previous year. Mr Gough appeared for the prosecution; the prisoner was undefended. The prisoner pleaded guilty. Mr Gough drew His Lordship's attention to the fact that the prisoner had purchased poison, which he had threatened to force down her throat. His Lordship doubted if anything could be made of the threat. Mr Smith, the governor of the city gaol proved four convictions against the prisoner, who was sentenced to twelve calendar months' hard labour.

Samuel Heritage, plasterer, 69, Cardigan-street, Jericho, was charged in December 1880 with assaulting his wife, Anna Maria Heritage. The complainant did not appear, and it was stated that she was unwell. Mr Mallam (the magistrates' clerk) read her statement saying that she and her husband had quarrelled. He struck her with his fist and badly blackened her face with no provocation. Heritage said she had used abusive language to him, Superintendent Head said he saw her the next day and she was in a dreadful state such as he had never seen. Both eyes were blacked and she could not see out of the right one. The mayor said if it had not been for the defendant's interceding for him when she laid the information, in all probability Heritage would have been sentenced to three months with hard labour. The magistrates now felt it to be their duty to send him to prison for fourteen days' hard labour. However, the following December Anna Maria Heritage was summoned by her husband, Samuel for assaulting him in November. She was bound over in five pounds and one surety of five pounds to keep the peace for six months.

From 1 September 1883: ASSAULT ON A WIFE – Henry Pledge, gas fitter, Bath-square, Bath-street, pleaded guilty to committing an aggravated assault on his wife. The wife said she wished to forgive her husband, if he would promise not to assault her again and to give up the drink. The prisoner said he would do so. The information of the wife was to the effect that the prisoner returned home from Bicester where he had been at work during the week and gave her five-pence. He was very drunk and went to bed, and later on, because there was no food in the cupboard he struck her on the nose. The prisoner said he had been locked up since the previous Friday and it had been such a lesson to him that he would not repeat the offence. The bench sentenced the prisoner to a month's hard labour and at the expiration of that time to be bound over to keep the peace for six months. The prisoner was removed, entreating that a fine might be imposed.

From 28 August 1886: ANOTHER ASSAULT ON A WIFE – Alfred Henry Allum, labourer, 4 King Street, Jericho, was charged on warrant with assaulting his wife, Elizabeth. The complainant said the prisoner came home drunk and upset her, pinched her arm, smacked her face, and they fell into the road together. On the previous Thursday he came home half drunk and refused to eat the food she had prepared; he swore at her, and smacked her face. Superintendent Head sad he saw the wife when she came to the station for protection. The wife said she had three children, and she had only had about seven shillings and sixpence from him since last September. Allum was sentenced to one month's hard labour and at the expiration to be bound over in ten shillings and one surety of five pounds to keep the peace for six months, and in default of finding the surety to undergo twenty-one days' hard labour further. The wife applied for a separation order, as she could not live with him, but the bench said they would give the prisoner another chance before taking this step.

NO PROSECUTRIX – 18 September 1886: James Allen, wheelwright, 2 Trinity-buildings, Blackfriars Road, was charged on warrant with committing an aggravated assault on his wife, Louisa. It was stated that the wife had been called three times, but did not answer, and the mayor said that possibly the parties had made it up and had agreed to live more harmoniously in the future than they had in the past. He, however, had appeared to have seriously assaulted his wife, but as she did not press the charge he would be allowed to go. He then left the dock.

From 9 July 1892: labourer James Gurden, of Church Street, St Ebbe's, was charged with assaulting his wife Elizabeth one Saturday afternoon. She deposed that her husband had followed her into Hanley's Tap and said, 'Holloa, ducky, how are you?' They drank some beer and on getting back home he started to abuse her, hit her, kicked her and got her down onto the ground. The prisoner stated that every Saturday his wife came home as drunk as a pig and she had not pawned her wedding ring in order to buy tea and sugar. She contested that she was never the worst for drink as she was forced to work too hard. Gurden contested that he had had difficulty in getting her home from the Tap and when he got there she had ripped the shirt off him, struck him, and almost throttled him. She replied that she had been a widow for fourteen years and had not even been married to Gurden for three months and that she wished that she were a widow again. Laughter in the court. Gurden stated that after they went home from their wedding, she pawned her wedding dress and lost the ticket and then pawned her wedding ring to buy drink. The mayor ordered Gurden to be bound over to keep the peace in the sum of five pounds and pay five shillings and sixpence costs or in default spend a week in prison. His wife asked the magistrates to grant a separation as she was sure she would never live with Gurden again, but they refused to grant it.

19

George Belcher was summoned at the city court by his wife for assault in September 1899. She claimed that he came home late one Sunday night and kicked her. Belcher took the stand and said that he had gone out about seven-thirty and returned two hours later. He was not drunk. When he arrived home his wife took a water bottle and banged him on the head with it. He did not go into a public house all day, he said, and had never assaulted her. He was bound over in the sum of five pounds to keep the peace for six months and ordered to pay six shillings reduced costs.

While there was no easily accessible means of divorce for ordinary people, couples tended to separate informally. The normal way was for the husband to leave. On 22 November 1890 *Jackson's* reported on a tramp called Margaret Day, who appeared in court with a baby in her arms, charged with being drunk, disorderly and begging in George Street on a Saturday night. PC Radburn related how the prisoner approached him in a drunken state to ask where she could get lodgings. When he told her it was too late, she became abusive and accused the policeman of pushing her, but this was denied. The prisoner said that her husband had deserted her and she was in great trouble. Chief Constable Head said that Day had two previous convictions and that she was a perfect nuisance in the town. She was fined two shillings and sixpence, six shillings and sixpence costs or seven days' hard labour.

On the other hand, some people could not bear to wait until they were free to remarry even though their spouses were still alive and in some cases living locally. In July 1858, Edward Eastick, otherwise Eastwick, a 45-year-old tile-maker, pleaded guilty to feloniously marrying Sarah Coxhill at St Thomas the Martyr church on 12 March 1855 while his wife, Dorothy Eastick, was still living. In passing sentence the judge told the prisoner that he had been convicted on his own confession of the crime of bigamy. Now, he said, 'where it was a more ecclesiastical fraud and the wife knew what she was doing, it was a more lenient offence but in this case he had induced an innocent woman to marry him on the false representation that he was a widower.' She had borne him two children who had no legal father, and the relationship between mother and child and father and son had been destroyed. He had done this woman a great injury and the judge felt that he would not be doing his duty if he did not impose a severe punishment, namely that he be imprisoned with hard labour for twelve calendar months.

DOMESTICS

At the Oxford Lent Assizes in March 1862, a 50-year-old labourer named William Tomkins pleaded guilty to feloniously marrying Elizabeth Bayless on 29 July 1861 while his first wife was still alive. The defence offered mitigating circumstances that might make for a more lenient sentence in that Tomkins had married his first wife in 1836, but they had been unhappy together and had no family. His wife had left him in 1849 and worked as a nurse in a union workhouse. In 1861 she had applied to the city magistrates for protection of her property on the grounds that her husband had deserted her when in fact she had deserted him. The magistrates made the order, which the prisoner had misunderstood, believing that he was now divorced and therefore free to remarry. He then married a widow with five children who naturally believed him to be divorced. The banns were read in the correct way and afterwards the couple married in St Paul's church. If she was aware of it, his first wife ignored the event. In passing sentence, the judge stated that there had been no question of deceit or a desire to take advantage of the woman. Under the circumstances the sentence of one month's imprisonment would be appropriate and as Tomkins had already been in prison for a week, he was to do hard labour for a further three weeks.

In October 1867 Henry James, a boat-builder, had been charged with bigamy but the case was dismissed due to lack of proof of a second marriage. However, he was also charged with assaulting his wife, Elizabeth. She was able to prove that she had followed her husband who struck her several times and threatened to throw her over the bridge into the stream below. He then ran off and spoke to another woman. He received three calendar months' imprisonment with hard labour and when that was over to enter into his own recognizance of fifty pounds to keep the peace.

This highly embarrassing notice appeared in *Jackson's* on 7 August 1869:

In Her Majesty's Court for Divorce and Matrimonial Causes
To HENRY WATKINS GREEN, now of late of Lincoln College, in the University of Oxford, Scholar,
TAKE NOTICE that a Citation bearing date the 19th day of June 1869 has issued under seal of Her Majesty's Court for Divorce and Matrimonial Causes at the instance of EMILY MARY GREEN of Bedford Villa, Summertown,

in the County of Oxford, citing you to appear in the said Court, then and there to answer her Petition, filed in the said Court, praying for a restitution of conjugal rights: and such Citation contains an intimation that, in default of your so doing, the Court will proceed to hear the said Petition proved in due course of law, and to pronounce sentence therein, your absence notwithstanding. – Dated this 29th day of July, 1869. Signed etc.

Frank Owen, a labour aged 32, died of a fit during a session on the treadwheel at Oxford Prison in July 1891 while serving a sentence for bigamy. At the inquest the coroner remarked that he had no reason to doubt that the deceased died from anything other than natural causes but it was nevertheless necessary to hold an enquiry on any person who died within the precincts of a prison. Owen had been convicted on 29 June and sentenced to three months' hard labour. The warders in charge of him had not noticed his experiencing any sort of difficulty while on the treadwheel. When he had started having a fit a telegraph was sent to his 'real' wife before he died; she replied the same way to say that she was unable to come and she also sent a letter saying that if she was wanted she would come to see him. The superintendent of police at Burford witnessed the fact that she had no way of getting to the inquest. The warder in charge at the time of Owen's death deposed that he had seen him fall backwards, clear of the treadwheel but he had not cried out or screamed. When he was taken back to his cell he said merely that his head ached. The following morning he was found to be unconscious and frothing at the mouth. The day after that he was no better and died about quarter to twelve in the morning, before medical assistance could reach him. The verdict was that 'the deceased had died from epilepsy.'

Children also suffered abuse and neglect in the home but it was not until the 1880s that societies, notably the National Society for the Prevention of Cruelty to Children (NSPCC), took offending parents to court. In November 1892 the NSPCC brought a case of cruelty against Edwin Woodward, a gardener from Sunnymead, North Oxford, for wilfully neglecting his two children, Edith and Gabriel, so as to be injurious to their health.

The prosecution stated that the children were almost dead of starvation despite the fact that their father earned about a shilling a week and that he certainly bought food and ate as much as he wanted himself. After putting aside a little for his wife and six children, he would lock the rest away so that they had no access to it. He had been doing this for about a year and had already been given a warning by the NSPCC the previous February.

An NSPCC inspector stated that he had visited the house on several occasions since then. The first time the baby, aged seven or eight weeks, 'was in a shocking state of starvation' and so he issued a certificate for it to be taken to the infirmary. He asked the defendant what food he had and was shown into the front room where he saw some that was not fit for a pig to eat, and was thrown away. The inspector advised Woodward to leave the food out rather that lock it away, but was told that he would do what he wanted with it and would continue to lock it up. The situation was similar on his later visits when tiny pieces of bread and a little condensed milk was in evidence as well as something in a pot, but 'it was such filth that he would not like to give it to pigs.'

The defendant said that he would like the food in the pot analyzed, which caused laughter in the court. He said that he himself had to put up with a bit of bread. Witnesses, including Mrs Woodward, stated that all that had been said about the food being locked away was correct. The children were usually very hungry during the day and never had new clothing. Her husband would fry meat for himself after she had gone to bed and on one occasion, when she asked him for food for the children, he put the meat away in the cupboard. He then broke the dishes, plates and tea things and tried to put out the fire with a bucket of water.

Woodward's local grocer said that he shopped with him most days and estimated that he bought enough bread to support a family every day. He was now refused credit as he owed more than nine pounds. Another witness said that Woodward had told her that he ate and drank all he could get, and the others had to have what he left. The defendant retorted that he locked the food away so that his family could not devour it all in one day and that he was, in fact, providing for them. He added: 'He that provideth not for his own household is worse than an infidel, and hath denied the truth.' Laughter in the court.

The magistrates decided that Woodward should be given the chance to make amends and officers of the NSPCC would keep a watch on the household. The case was to be adjourned for a month in the hope of future improvements. He was then charged with not sending two of his other children, Heber and Esther, to school regularly.

William Galloway and Emily Carter of Cousins's lodging house in St Thomas's were charged with wilfully neglecting a child named William Carter who had been in their charge in July and August 1892. They pleaded guilty. A surgeon deposed that a 19-month-old child named Carter was brought to the workhouse with numerous bruises on its head and body, two scabs on the nose and a missing tooth. Both eyes were blackened. It was very thin and emaciated, weighing only twelve and a half pounds whereas it should have been over twenty pounds. It now weighed nineteen pounds and had been restored to health with normal food and cleanliness rather than medication.

Galloway claimed that he knew nothing about any ill treatment of the child but added that its mother had fits and had dropped it. She admitted that she had given it a 'smack or two on its little arms' when it was very cross and she made its little mouth bleed through dropping it when she had a fit. The mayor said that the magistrates had found the prisoners guilty of 'most cruel, determined, and persistent misconduct towards the child, and they had moreover neglected it to such an extent that it was a great marvel that they were not accused of a more serious crime.' Galloway and Carter were imprisoned with hard labour for three months.

George and Annie Cox, a cabinet-maker and his wife of Beef Lane, St Ebbe's, were charged in March 1899, at the instance of the NSPCC, with neglecting their children Irene aged 9, John, 7, Lilian, 6 and Louisa aged 5 in a manner likely to cause them unnecessary suffering over the past six months. They pleaded not guilty.

Cox, the prosecution stated, earned good wages but was handicapped by his wife 'who was a drunken woman and had pawned his tools.' Inspector Cole of the NSPCC related how he had visited Cox's house where he found three of the children involved. The room was filthy with decomposing food on the table. John was sitting in the grate, soiled and emaciated. Louisa was suffering badly from rickets and was also filthy and emaciated as was Lilian who was wearing a dirty frock and was crawling with vermin. The eldest child then came into the house with beer for their mother. 'The effluvia from the children was most offensive.' The parents and children all slept in the same room and their bedding was stiff with dirt.

He questioned Mrs Cox and asked if poverty was to blame for conditions in the home, to which she replied that it was not as her husband earned good wages. The witness said that he continually saw the woman drunk and she was drunk during the inspector's visit. Cox said that he had expected this outcome because of his wife's condition. He then produced a number of pawn tickets that his wife had been given in exchange for his tools without his consent.

The children were removed to the workhouse where they were sent to the isolation ward. Thanks to the previous good character of Cox he would be fined forty shillings and twenty-two shillings and sixpence costs, or one calendar month's hard labour, with a warning that he could no long shirk the responsibility of caring for his children. As regards his wife, the bench decided unanimously to send her to prison for four calendar months with hard labour.

Under the Elementary Education Act of 1880, schooling was compulsory until the age of 10. *Jackson's* carries numerous accounts of court cases brought against parents for not sending their children to school, another more subtle kind of mistreatment.

Chapter 4

Robbery and Theft

On 27 September 1375, a jury stated that over the previous Christmas a cleric named John Taylor had stolen a quilt and a double sheet worth twenty-six shillings and three-pence from townsman John Windsor. On Easter Monday he robbed the Carmelite prior, Brother John, of three coverlets, and three testers and curtains worth five pounds. On the day before Easter he had taken two little cloaks called almuces worth thirteen shillings and four-pence belonging to William Marchaunt from Leadenporch Hall.

From 12 May 1388: two town bailiffs heard how the night after Easter, John Curteys, William Harbuigh, David Kam, William Crun, Philip Mayheu, David Krane, Morice Lowys, John Burton, William Willerby, a cleric named Thomas Sherman and others, broke into the shop of John Spycer, tailor, in St Martin's parish where they stole coloured cloth. They then stole four shillings and eight-pence from William Palmer's cellar. The jurymen stated that these were common thieves and added that Matilda Deye, Rosa Webbe and Elena Lotlevyn had sheltered them from the authorities previously, knowing about their crimes. They added that Isabella Whyte, an Irishwoman, had stolen John Styvyngton's dagger worth three shillings and four-pence and later two silver spoons worth two shillings from John Dysson's house. Also that Welshman Lodwycue Bonethyng stole a dagger worth three shillings and four-pence from John Gwyneie.

On 1 September 1389, the jury deposed that one night Walter Gum, manciple of Checker Hall, Simon Coventre, manciple of St Edmund Hall, Robert Wastel, Robert Hethe, Nicholas Tourseye and John Lude, gardener, along with others unknown robbed Robert Maydem, manciple of St Lawrence Hall, of a wax candle worth five shillings. They beat Robert up so badly that he nearly died. The jury added that these and others, armed with axes and other implements, cut down the doors, windows and stalls of the Prior of St Frideswide and Hugh de Wyndle and tried to enter and rob their houses. These and other offenders broke into William Bergeveny's shop in St Martin's parish and stole fifteen lamb skins worth three shillings.

The Great University Burglary took place on 21 February 1544, when it lost most of its treasures. Richard Raunce and John Stanshawe, armed with a hammer, an iron bar and some pincers, arrived at St Mary the Virgin, broke into the chests and made off with plate and other valuables. They returned eleven days later for more plunder including the university's entire supply of cash. They were both soon caught, sent for trial and sentenced to death. However, the university had no cash to pay its legal expenses so a collection of gold and silver oddments was hastily made and the Master of University College, Leonard Hutcheson, sold it off to raise funds. The total collected was 389½ ounces of which he sold 377 ounces for £71 14s 5½d. Three gold rings, a brooch and pieces of broken drinking bowls remained and he gave these to the proctors. Raunce was said to be an Oxford scholar and Stanshawe was described as 'of Oxford, gentleman', relevant because Raunce was pardoned after the intervention of another member of the university but Stanshawe's fate is unrecorded in the University Archives.

On 19 October 1687 between midnight and one, twelve armed men entered Gloucester Hall's main gate, presumably they were let in by someone already inside. Using a large piece of wood they opened the window bars, made their way into the rooms by candlelight, approached the beds and tied up the hands and feet of the occupants, except for the Principal, Dr Eaton. They stole six or seven pieces of silver plate belonging to the hall and Dr Eaton's porringers, spoons, trenchers, rings and other jewellery, and his daughters' silk petticoats and waistcoats. They then went downstairs, ate whatever they could find, downed three or four bottles of wine and drank to the young ladies' health. Dr Eaton's losses were estimated at £300. This unfortunate man had already lost several sons, only his daughters were left, and had previously been robbed twice in two or three years.

From 22 May 1784: sieve-maker Joseph Taylor was sentenced to transportation for seven years for stealing leather but managed to escape from prison. His wife and mother were gaoled instead on suspicion of helping him to get away. At the July quarter sessions that year, Joseph Peere was sentenced to death for stealing money and a shirt marked 'RS' from a box in the house of Mrs Williams at the King's Head Inn, the property of Samuel Smith.

In March 1786, Joseph Reynolds, coachman to William Bolton, was committed to the castle for robbing his master at the Cross Inn. He had broken open a box in the bedroom and stolen thirty guineas in gold, the property of Bolton. Reynolds was burnt in the hand and discharged.

Benjamin Petty appeared at the mayor's court in June 1830 along with six others then unknown, charged with having taken a boat and entered a garden belonging to Thomas Hands, 'an industrious poor man with a large family', and stolen all his cabbages. Petty and three others were spotted by Joseph Beesley while he was rowing his punt between four and five o'clock the previous Sunday morning. He saw Petty and three others in Hands' garden pulling up the cabbages. Then they got into a boat but when they saw Beesley, ran away leaving the cabbages in the boat. After offering an unsuccessful alibi, Petty was fined five pounds with costs; in default of payment he was sent to the treadmill for two months.

In September 1830 Frederick Seymour was charged with stealing a silver watch, a glazier's diamond and a silver spoon belonging to Richard Smith of St Aldates. The prisoner, 'a genteel looking young man', had been noticed in a state of great distress by Smith. He described himself as the son of Captain Seymour, formerly of Christ Church. The kindly Smith took him into his house and found him work only to be repaid by Seymour stealing the articles. He was traced to Abingdon with them still in his possession and sent for trial.

Thomas Winter appeared before the mayor in February 1832 on suspicion of stealing a pair of 'kerseymere trowsers'. Police Officer Keates stated that he had seen the prisoner offering them for sale for four shillings at a second-hand shop in St Peter-le-Bailey. Believing them not to be his to sell, Keates stopped him and 'took the trowsers into his custody.' Winter claimed that they had been given to him in Woodstock by a man called Henderson but Keates managed to trace them to city surgeon Charles Wingfield who appeared in court and identified them as his property that had gone missing on the day they were found in the prisoner's possession. Winter was sent for trial at the next sessions.

One Sunday morning in February 1832, two police officers were informed that poultry and other items had been stolen from Mr Curr, a publican at South Hinksey. On investigating, the officers found some feathers scattered around the premises of William Harris, a reputed thief from St Thomas's parish. In his bedroom they came across more feathers, recently plucked as well as heads and wings, still with the feathers on. They arrested Harris and having found out that a notorious character, the appropriately named Charles Cock, had been seen with Harris, immediately arrested Cock and found more of the stolen property on him. The two men appeared before the mayor and when Mr Curr identified his property under oath, and other evidence was given placing the pair in the area about the time of the robbery, they were sent for trial at the next sessions.

At the city sessions in October 1847 it was announced that a potentially distressing case was about to come up as the prisoner was disabled. This was Henry Trump, 'a very respectable-looking man, deaf and dumb', who pleaded guilty (in writing), to the charge of stealing a gold pencil case belonging to Robert Rixon Stephens. Mr Stephens asked that the court be lenient with Trump and the recorder in passing sentence (in writing) noted that as he believed this to be his first offence, and taking into consideration that he had already been in custody for almost two months, the court sentenced him to return to prison for a further week.

In September 1855 James Cattle, 'one of the professors of "the manly art of self-defence"', who had been 'a very prominent personage at the sparring booth in St Giles's Fair' appeared before the bench charged with assaulting a North-West Railway policeman named Joseph Brooks and stealing a purse containing four sovereigns and fifteen or sixteen shillings in silver. Brooks stated that on his way home from work, when he was in St Giles, the prisoner and three other men accosted him and Cattle knocked him down. The others attacked him and took the purse and money and then ran off in different directions. Brooks went after Cattle who was soon captured by a university policeman but the other three escaped with the money. Cattle denied the charge, saying that he had never seen Brooks before, but the magistrates committed him for trial at the next city sessions.

Mary Ann Brown, a common prostitute aged 26, was charged in October 1855 with stealing fourteen shillings from Alexander Parrott. She pleaded not guilty. Between midnight and one o'clock one Sunday morning, Parrott met the prisoner in New Road and went with her to Bullocks (Bulwarks) Alley 'where an improper intercourse took place between them.' Not long afterwards, Parrott looked for his purse containing a half-sovereign and four shillings. He accused Brown of robbing him and took her to the police station where she was searched but nothing was found. The policeman then searched the part of the alley where the pair had been and found the purse and money deliberately hidden under a door where only a small part of it could be seen. The prisoner declined to comment. The jury found her guilty and she was sentenced to three months' imprisonment with hard labour.

In January 1858, Ellen Ludlow, a prostitute aged 24, was charged with stealing two sovereigns and other coins from the person of schoolmaster John Sixsmith in Paradise Square the previous December. Sixsmith related how he had been on his way home and had got as far as Castle Street when he was accosted by Ludlow who said, 'Master, give us half-a-pint of beer,' to which he replied that he had nothing to give her. When he reached Paradise Square he stopped to relieve himself against a wall and while he was doing so Ludlow came up behind him, threw one arm round his neck and with her other hand started going through his pocket. Sixsmith struggled with her and landed in the middle of the road. He got straight back up again and realized that he had been robbed. He accused her and said that if she would return the money he would drop the matter. She denied having the cash but as a policeman came along and arrested her, Sixsmith went on home. Ludlow said that she had no money and when searched was found to have one penny on her. The jury returned a guilty verdict and the recorder said that although she had appeared in court on several previous occasions, she had never been convicted so he would treat this as the first offence and she was sent to prison for twelve months.

In July 1857 Harriet Ann Carter, aged 40, pleaded guilty to stealing two pounds of bacon from Grimbly Hughes and Dewe's grocery shop. The defence pleaded mitigating circumstances as Carter had nine children and her husband was confined to bed. The recorder's response was to sentence her to two months' imprisonment for stealing some gloves the previous June and because she had not mended her ways, he considered that the children would be better off without such a bad example for a mother. As she had already been in prison for ten weeks he ordered a further three months in gaol.

A respectably dressed young man who gave his name as John Swaine, his occupation as tailor and stated that he would be coming into property, was charged in August 1861 with stealing a silver watch belonging to

William Ward on the racecourse on Port Meadow. 'The prisoner, on being brought into court, assumed a very penitential air, crying and protesting his innocence in a most confident manner, and ended up by going on his knees and with clasped hands, imploring the magistrates to forgive him, vowing that he had never been in prison before.' Shortly afterwards, however, he calmed down and pleaded guilty to the charge. The mayor replied that there was no doubt that he was an habitual thief and that he should be sent for trial. In the meantime he was to have his photograph taken in order to gather more information about him. The prosecutor stated that Swaine had attracted notice on the racecourse when he pushed between him and another man; he was shaking as if he were suffering from palsy. After a few minutes the prosecutor heard a snap like a pipe breaking and looking at his waistcoat he found that his watch had disappeared. He grabbed hold of Swaine and the watch was discovered on the ground where Swaine had dropped it between his legs on realizing that he had been caught red-handed. He was taken into custody prior to appearing at the sessions.

In January 1867 a labourer, Henry White aged 35, pleaded guilty to stealing fourteen pounds of cheese belonging to Francis Hewitt. William Thompson, a 24-year-old iron-turner who was charged with being an accomplice, pleaded not guilty. White was seen taking the cheese which was later found in Thompson's possession. He was also found guilty of a previous conviction, still in force, for stealing a coat. White stated that at the time of the theft he was quite destitute or he would not have done this. The cheese had been positioned about five yards in front of the shop door. The recorder commented that tradesmen were certainly offering temptation to thieves 'to expose their goods unnecessarily' although of course this was no excuse. Thompson already had six convictions and was sentenced to five years' penal servitude and White to three months' imprisonment.

On 12 February 1870 George Walters pleaded guilty to stealing a pork pie from the Cornmarket shop of Edward Horn. In company with another tramp, he went into the shop to beg and while the manager, John Horn, had his back turned, Walters snatched a pork pie worth one shilling and sixpence. He was spotted before he had had time 'to eat the purloined dainty' and arrested. He was sent to prison for ten days.

John Bruce, a boy of about 13 was charged in September 1870 with robbing the till of Edward Radbone, grocer, of Clarendon Street in

Jericho, in whose shop he was working. He was seen going to the till and taking money from it. He pleaded guilty and was sent to gaol for a week where he received six strokes with a birch rod.

A married woman named Emma Bull, of Park Passage, Holywell, was charged in June 1881 with stealing three pound fifteen ounces of beef worth two shillings and sixpence from Robert Alden's shop in the Covered Market one evening. PC Butler stated that he was called to the market where he saw the prisoner with something under her arm. When questioned, she answered that what she had got she had paid for but refused to show him what it was. Finally she agreed on condition that he would move further along the avenue. He saw the piece of beef and when she refused to say where she had bought it, threatened to charge her with shoplifting. He took her to Alden's where she said she had bought it from one of the men there but Mr Alden said it had been there ten minutes earlier and handed her over to the constable. He dragged her to the police station where it was found she also had a piece of bacon which she swore she had bought from Radbone's. On reaching the cells, she asked if she had been seen taking the beef, to which he answered that she had. She then begged him to return to the market and plead with Mr Alden to be lenient because of her children. In court, Robert Alden identified the piece of meat as one that had been on a block outside his shop. The prisoner stated that she had bought it for one shilling and sixpence from a lad at the shop, and thought it a bargain. Mr Alden retorted that there was no lad around at the time. When asked to identify him she became confused and asked him to be lenient with her. Bull, 'who seemed to feel her position very acutely' was let off with a fine of one guinea or twenty-one days' hard labour.

In February 1880 a labourer named Daniel Holland was charged with stealing from Frederick Butterfield's butcher's shop in New Road. He made off with a pound of pork sausages worth ten-pence. A boy named Josiah Coppock said that he saw the prisoner take the sausages from a board. He had told Mr Butterfield but he was not able to leave the shop, so the boy followed Holland to Carfax where he informed a policeman, who arrested Holland. PC Purnell confirmed that the boy had pointed the prisoner out to him and he had apprehended him as he was eating the raw sausages as fast as he could. He was also the worst for drink. Holland pleaded guilty and as he already had a conviction for vagrancy he was sentenced to a calendar month's hard labour.

At the vice-chancellor's court in March 1885, Frederick William Young, a watch and clock cleaner of Luther Street, St Aldate's, was charged with theft from the Queen's College Hall, in between January and March. He took eight silver table forks, five silver soup spoons and eleven silver dessert spoons valued at twenty pounds, the property of the provost and Fellows of the college. In the absence of the vice-chancellor, the chairman of the county quarter sessions said that the prisoner would be remanded in the County Hall a few days later when substantial evidence regarding the charge would be produced.

From *Jackson's* of 19 December 1885: at the police court Francis Earle Suckling and some bronze coins. An undergraduate at St Mary Hall, was charged with stealing a cashbox containing two five-pound Old Bank notes, one pound ten shillings in gold, seventeen shillings and sixpence in silver, threepenny piece and some bronze coins. This belonged to another junior member, Arthur Spearling who notified the police of the theft as well as notifying many local tradesmen and giving them the numbers of the banknotes. Emma Kerry of Church Street, Holywell a college bed-maker told the court that she found the cashbox in a coal bin near Spearling's rooms; it had been broken open. She returned it to the owner.

Jeweller John Rogers, of 37 High Street, related how the accused had been to his shop wanting to buy some salts, a cross and a sovereign purse totalling twelve shillings, for which he handed over a five-pound Old Bank note bearing the number of one of those notified as stolen so he called the police. PC Miller went to the shop and took the note along with another that the accused took out of his pocket. When told that they had been stolen from St Mary Hall, he replied that he had found them on a staircase. PC Prior searched Suckling's rooms and found a hammer hidden there. On it were traces of gilt from where it had been used to wrench the lid off.

Because Suckling had left Oxford for St Ives, a remand was requested and granted, the prisoner being bailed in two sureties of £100 each from the Principal and Vice-Principal of St Mary Hall. At the next session, during which the owner of the box was called Sperling, the magistrates were unanimous that the evidence was sufficient to warrant the prisoner for trial at the quarter sessions with an increased bail of £200 each from the two sureties. Eventually, Suckling was found guilty but the jury recommended leniency because of his previous good character. However, the court was adjourned while a suitable punishment was considered. Towards the end of January, there was much debate about the prisoner's ability to cope with hard labour and in the end, he was sent to prison for three months without it, backdated to when he was first detained.

In October 1886 John Eastwood, a tramp, was charged with begging in Bridge Street, Osney one Sunday afternoon and also with later stealing a piece of beef worth sixpence from Charlotte Linstead in Southmoor Road. PC Veary said that he saw Eastwood go to two doors, where he was given something at each. The accused then started to sing and when the PC looked into his basket he found that it contained meat, pudding, cheese, dripping and bread and he had two shillings and tuppence in bronze in his pockets. Eastwood denied that he was begging but was singing to earn money for his night's lodging. Sarah Walker, Mrs Linstead's servant, said that Eastwood had been at the door asking if her mistress could help him as he had a wife and four children who were starving. When she replied that Mrs Eastwood could do nothing to help him he became abusive. She had just put the lodger's steak on the table in the front room, and after Eastwood had left the lodger complained that the steak was nowhere to be found. She identified the prisoner from his clothing and the basket. Eastwood denied this charge but the bench believed that he was guilty and he was sentenced to seven days for the begging and twenty-one days for the theft.

Sarah Henderson, a prostitute of Caroline Street, St Clement's, was charged at the Oxford city police court in November 1889 with stealing an academic cap worth five shillings and nine-pence, the property of Harold Arthur Pollock of Keble College – she was discharged.

Michael Ryan, James Brewer and Albert Reynolds, tramps, were charged in April 1893 regarding a theft from the back yard of a house in South Street, Osney. Their haul consisted of two men's cotton shirts, five worsted socks, one pair of cotton socks, and one pair of worsted stockings belonging to Henry Shirley and worth five shillings and sixpence. Mrs Shirley said that these items had been hung out in the garden all night but in the morning they had vanished. There were footprints in the garden and those of surrounding neighbours. The magistrates remarked that they would have to pass through three gardens and climb a high wall to get at the clothes.

Thomas Meynell, an assistant at Grainge's pawnbrokers said that Brewer had brought in a bundle containing shirts, saying that one belonged to his brother and the other was his own. The sum of one shilling and sixpence was advanced on them. PC Furnage said that he had searched the 'Never Despair' lodging house in St Thomas's but found none of the items. He afterwards arrested Brewer and charged him with the theft. Brewer then claimed that he had pawned the two shirts for a man in the lodging house. When searched, he was seen to be wearing odd socks identical to those stolen. Ryan claimed that he had bought the things from a man in the street while Reynolds claimed no knowledge of the other men. However, a witness noticed that he was wearing Brewer's cap. The footsteps in the gardens corresponded with the boots of Ryan and Brewer but not Reynolds. After a good deal of false claims and explanations, Mrs Shirley identified the socks as her husband's at which the prisoners had no more to say. Reynolds had been convicted in 1891 for stealing a pair of boots but there was no evidence against him on this occasion. Ryan and Brewer were sent to prison for three weeks' hard labour.

In December 1894 James Henry Atkins, an 11-year-old schoolboy of Burrows's Yard and James Ernest Ward, aged 14, an errand boy from Friars Street, were charged on remand with stealing a quantity of elastic gaiters belonging to Cape and Company in St Ebbe's Street. They were also charged with stealing a boy's cloth cap worth sixpence, the property of G.W. Turner, the same day. Charles Ettham, assistant to Mr Turner of Cowley Road, stated that he had hung out a number of caps outside the shop and found that two of them were missing the next morning. He identified the cap produced as evidence as one of these. Henry Lewis of St Ebbe's similarly identified the gaiters as being the kind sold in his shop but added that he had no wish to press charges. Each of the boys protested that the other had taken the articles. Ward was sent to a reformatory for four years and Atkins received six strokes with a birch rod.

Chapter 5

Riotous Behaviour

Although the Oxford area has seldom been troubled by threats of serious rebellion or invasion or suffered serious war damage, it has a history of disturbances and strife. An early example took place in 1002 when, because of repeated demands for Danegeld and a series of Viking invasions, King Aethelred issued an edict, stating that it was not illegal to kill any Danes living in England. The edict, however, was most unfair to those Danes who had settled peaceably and raised families in England.

On 13 November, St Brice's Day, members of Oxford's Danish community were forced to take refuge in the priory church of St Frideswide, the precursor of today's cathedral, which the townspeople set on fire. Among the dead were Gunnhild, the sister of the King of Denmark, and her family. A royal charter refers to the Danes as 'sprouting like cockle among the wheat' and states that they were killed 'by a most just extermination'. Furthermore, they had ruined doors of St Frideswide when they frantically tried to escape the flames. The loss of books and damage to the church are evidently felt to be more important than the lives of those who perished. The charter also includes the information that Aethelred felt responsible for the rebuilding of the church 'with God's aid'. In rapid retribution, Sweyn Forkbeard burnt the town to the ground.

A series of incidents continued this tradition of violence. In 1209, for example, a scholar who was accused of killing a townswoman, who may or may not have been a prostitute, escaped from the town. Nevertheless, the authorities hanged several scholars who had lodged with him, but had not been involved in the murder. This had the effect of bringing the university to a standstill as lectures stopped and scholars left Oxford for more peaceful locations among which was Cambridge.

The townspeople were ingenious in finding ways of quarrelling with the students. One night in 1248 they killed a scholar of noble blood whom they had come across near St Martin's church on Carfax. They assaulted him for no reason, firstly hitting him and then using lumps of offal from the butchers' stalls. He was smeared all over as he tried to escape while others pelted him with stones and all sorts of filth from the street. At last he fell, half dead before the door of All Saints church from where he was rescued and taken to his own home, where he died three days later. The city bailiffs allowed his murderers to walk at large through the streets, treated them as normal and under armed guard escorted them to St Mary's church where they were allowed to remain safely in sanctuary.

The university was most indignant and refused to hold any lectures and announced that unless this crime was duly reported and dealt with, they would stop any studying in the town. Furthermore, they would not allow the dead body to be buried until they had an answer from the king about the affair. Because he could not prove who had done the deed, the Bishop of Lincoln ordered an official to come to Oxford immediately and pronounce a public excommunication against anyone breaching the peace of the church and university by setting about a scholar and killing him. This included anyone who aided and abetted such behaviour. The proclamation was read out in all of the Oxford churches with lighted candles and bells tolling. Then the official was to convene a jury to investigate the murder and to publish also an agreement made between the university and the town drawn up by the papal legate who was at the time residing at Osney Abbey. Anybody found guilty would incur the full penalty of the law. It was said that the Sheriff of Oxfordshire, acting on a royal writ, seized all the goods of one of the town's vintners, an accomplice in the murder and fined him by removing most of his stock of wine. The scholars expressed their ongoing resentment by summoning Robert Wells, bailiff of the North Gate Hundred and a well-known challenger of the university's rights and privileges. They swore an oath to the effect that they would immediately shut up the schools and suspend all academic procedures unless justice was done regarding their implacable enemy.

As the fourteenth century wore on, due to a number of factors that affected most of the country, the quality of Oxford life worsened, as did the relationship between Town and Gown. The result was another exodus in 1330, this time to Lincolnshire where another university grew up at Stamford. However the situation in Oxford remained fraught. On 10 February 1355, the feast of St Scholastica, a horrific incident began that would have repercussions on Oxford life for half a millennium. It started in a common enough way with an argument over the quality of the ale at the Swyndlestock Tavern on Carfax and ended as a bloodbath, arguably the blackest time in Oxford's history. The affray continued relentlessly for two days and two nights with property being pillaged and set on fire. When it came to an end, sixty-three students and about half that number of townspeople had been killed. Edward III intervened in the dispute that resulted in a charter being granted in favour of the university to the great humiliation of the town. The mayor and burgesses were ordered to attend an annual service at St Mary the Virgin on the anniversary of the massacre and pay out a penny for each student who lost their lives.

One account, apparently written by a member of the university, reads:

> 'February 10th 1738. This being St Scholastica's Day, a certain number of the principal Burgesses did Publickly pay each one penny in token of their submission to the orders and rights of the University. The occasion of this custom and offering was a barbarous and bloody outrage committed by the citizens in the reign of Edward the Third against the persons and goods of several scholars which drew a great and just amercement upon the criminals. The City pretended they were not able to pay the fine without their utter ruin and did humbly pray and at last obtained a Mitigation from the University an annual payment of 100 Marks was then accepted and this by farther of the University was changed into a small yearly acknowledgement viz that the Mayor and 62 such townsmen as had been sworn that year to preserve the privileges of the University should yearly upon this day repair to St Mary's Church and should then and there offer 63 pence in memory of the barbarous murder of 63 innocent scholars.'

The ceremony involved the vice-chancellor, proctors, registrar and the Vicar of St Mary's assembling in the chancel to wait for the mayor and bailiffs and citizens to a total of sixty-three to represent the number of scholars said to have been killed in 1355. In the course of the ceremony sixty-three-pence, normally in small silver coins, were presented by one of the bailiffs and received and counted by the senior proctor. After this the Town party left and the money was distributed among the vicar and the bedels.

In 1825 the mayor flatly refused to comply with this ancient edict and at a convocation held in February 1855, the university seal was put on a document that released Town from the St Scholastica's Day disgrace. The city 'returned the warmest acknowledgments to the University for this Act of Grace.' This was not entirely unexpected for the previous year the mayor and bailiffs had made up their minds to boycott the ceremony in St Mary's. In 1955 on the 600th anniversary, an honorary doctorate was conferred by the university on the mayor at the time as a very belated peace offering.

In 1378 there was a revolt at St Frideswide's Priory; it is recorded in document reference SC8/215/10740 in the National Archives. The prior, John de Dodeford, complained to the king and council that he had been elected prior with royal assent confirmed by the Bishop of Lincoln and received the appropriate secular possessions and properties from the king. Dodeford had come to London because of false accusations made against him back in Oxford. A number of the canons had ordained a man named Wallingford as prior in Dodeford's place and were wasting food and other commodities in the priory. They had installed armed men and archers as if the building were a fortress or castle. Dodeford requested that a commission be sent to remove them, to restore him as prior and to punish the rebel canons and also that writs be issued forbidding the mayor, bailiffs and townsmen to aid and abet these canons. Sympathizers of both city and university found numerous ways in which to express their opinions on current social, economic and political issues as the following selection shows.

On 6 January 1793, 'An effigy of the notorious revolutionary and infidel writer "Tom Paine" was burnt at night on Carfax, the usual scene of rows and bonfire.' There was a bonfire, kept ablaze by frequent contributions of faggots, hurdles, old doors, tar barrels and anything else that would burn. As it was out of Term and therefore almost exclusively a Town affair, the magistrates, who sympathized with the sentiments expressed, turned a rather short-sighted eye.

The Riot Act was read in the presence of the vice-chancellor on Carfax in 1798, the occasion being protests against the price of bread. These were repeated in 1799 and again in 1800. Despite liberal handouts and the distribution of soup, the poor were in great distress from the high price of bread which was often of inferior quality together with 'the other countless trials of poverty' and this led to violence. Bakers' shops were targeted by noisy mobs of angry men, women and children, driven by hunger.

On 1 October 1800, *Jackson's* wrote:

'We are greatly concerned to state that the peace and good order of the city were again broken in upon on Wednesday evening, when the mob proceeded about the principal streets in a very riotous and tumultuous manner, breaking the lamps and windows of several of the inhabitants, and what was a great aggravation of their offence, and manifested a most wicked and malignant design, a stone was aimed at the head of a dignified and much respected member of the University, which happily only struck his cap, without doing further mischief. – The mayor, accompanied by Mr Weston and Mr Parsons [two magistrates] and a considerable number of the most respectable citizens, hastened, upon the first alarm, to the scene of tumult and by their exertions soon restored the peace of the place, after taking two of the most disorderly into custody; and the next day the Corporation published a hand bill, offering a reward of twenty guineas for the apprehension of any of the ringleaders and abettors.'

One of the proctors 'involved himself, and with him the whole University, in a squabble with the City, by carrying off to the *Castle* (as was the practice in those days when there were no Police-rooms) a quiet, but stubborn, old man who refused to "go home" at the Proctor's bidding, at the close of a *Town and Gown row*. Legal proceedings against the Proctor followed; but the case being *claimed* by the University to be decided in its own Court, the poor townsman relinquished any further proceedings.' The man's name was Bayliss, he was aged 70, and he was kept imprisoned two nights and a day because he refused 'to be sent home like a dog to his kennel.'

It would be a mistake to believe that Town and Gown clashes had been done away with by the abolition of the St Scholastica's Day penance. The mid-nineteenth century is littered with references to such confrontations. The favourite occasion for this was the Fifth of November or Bonfire

Night, and contemporary literature, both fact and fiction, gives graphic descriptions of damage to property and persons, arrests and appearances before the proctors, who, at that period, walked the streets of Oxford at nights in search of wrongdoers. Bonfire Night vandalism (or, as it is sometimes called in Oxford 'letting off steam'), continued well into the middle of the twentieth century when cars were to be seen suspended from Magdalen Bridge, pushed into the river, or occasionally set alight.

On 10 February 1840 Queen Victoria was married to her beloved Albert. The royal wedding was celebrated throughout the country, but in Oxford, G.V. Cox tells us that 'a bad spirit abroad at this time, and the lower orders of Oxford had not quite escaped its influence.' Confrontations with Gown took place in the streets with shouting and skirmishing. 'The gutters, however, did not "run with blood" indeed there was little more than the noise and show of fight, and the only red fluid was that which went down the guttur [gullet] of individuals.'

The 1840s continued to be a decade of disturbances for Gown as well as Town. On 26 June 1843 the annual Encaenia, or honorary degree ceremony, took place as usual in the Sheldonian Theatre. The junior proctor of that year was made very well aware of the dislike of undergraduate members of the university who insisted on interrupting the ceremony. As Cox puts it 'one continued storm of yelling and hissing was kept up by the rioters.' It became necessary for the honorary degrees to be conferred 'in dumb show. The Creweian Oration was read, but not a word of it was heard.' In the end, the vice-chancellor dissolved the meeting before it was finished.

On the night of 16 November 1867 more than 300 freshmen were attracted by the idea of a Fifth of November brawl. Their opponents were a number of foreign workmen 'even more desirous of a share in skirmish of worldwide celebrity' and highly flammable material was in evidence. The early evening had been so quiet that the authorities assumed nothing was going to happen and that the university police and the special constables who had been sworn in would have little to occupy them.

However, several hundred undergraduates appeared on the streets after the finish of a concert at the town hall and quickly came to blows with people whom *Jackson's* calls 'roughs' as a continuation of fights that had taken place earlier in the week.

A large number of Christ Church gentlemen were being pursued down St Aldates to the college's Fair Gate when they turned on their attackers. One, who went by the name of 'Doubtful' was dragged into Tom Quad and towards the fountain to be ducked then kicked out of the door. Outrages were committed by both Town and Gown.

The crowd then received reinforcements from the Covered Market which had been open because it was Saturday. Having been among the provisions on sale there, people noticed the high prices and started to grumble about them, particularly bread; even though that of corn was falling, the bakers had refused to lower the price of a quarter loaf by as much as a halfpenny. This grievance added fuel to the flames.

To make matters worse, Balliol College staff had gone on strike over the fact that their wages had not been increased to cover the price of food; they had already done so the previous May. Their hours were cut because of the shorter days and their wages accordingly. They were losing two hours' work and their dinner time reduced to thirty minutes while their tea break had been stopped altogether.

Between midnight and one in the morning, the proctor, accompanied by six or seven bulldogs, went to the house of the newly elected mayor, Alderman Carr to make him aware of the state that the city was in. By that time, all the members of university were back in their colleges and all that were left in the streets were townsmen. When the mayor took to the streets he was confronted by some 600 to 800 people 'in the most excited state imaginable'. He asked them to follow him to Carfax where he would address them but when they got there he could not make himself heard or even seen. He begged them to disperse offering to listen to their grievances on the Monday morning, however if they persisted with their vandalism they could expect the magistrates to deal with them. Most then went away, many shaking the mayor's hand as he 'passed down the human avenue.'

Nevertheless some hotheads continued to riot and smashed the windows of Alderman Grubb's baker's and corn-dealer's premises in Queen Street and Cornmarket and the streets were not cleared until about three in the morning.

In the course of the rioting several people were badly injured and many taken to chemists' shops for treatment to gashes on their heads and faces. One of the university policemen was knocked down and deliberately kicked in the head; fortunately he was well enough to go back to work on the Tuesday. Meetings were held by both Town and Gown authorities, the latter going as far as gating the whole undergraduate body in residence and allowing those in lodgings to be sworn in as special constables. The Militia and the City Rifle Corps agreed to cooperate with the civic authorities.

There were threats of a raid on the Great Western Goods Station where it was rumoured thousands of tons of corn were being stored to raise the price of bread. As the station was over the county border in Berkshire, magistrates from that county sent more than twenty special constables and the railway company contributed a number of their employees in the same capacity.

Meanwhile, the mayor had telegraphed the Home Secretary to say that the magistrates feared a riot in the city at night but everything had been done to cope with this. He ended with a query as to whom he should apply if it became necessary to bring in the military. The reply was that two companies of Grenadier Guards had been dispatched from Windsor to Oxford. The Corn Exchange was prepared as accommodation for them using beds from the workhouse and gaol. They duly arrived and were welcomed with food and drink.

An unusually thick fog which threw a pall over the city increased the sense of fear and chaos and, as *Jackson's* put it, 'gave an immunity to crime.' However, although the number of people who had turned out gave the appearance of a mob, most were only there out of curiosity. Those who were there to defend the city made an impressive show and had to deal with little more than insults. Occasionally troublemakers tried to make a ruckus but they were soon dealt with.

More of Grubb's windows were smashed and about 150 men attacked his shop in St Clements which was barricaded with bags of flour. About 200 more, including many who were 'recognized as respectable citizens' made their way up to Summertown, stoning houses and smashing lamps as they went. It became clear that their target was Grubb's private residence. As they tried to scale the wall, a properly armed and disciplined constabulary force attacked the rioters who instantly dispersed and ran off into the foggy night.

Back in the city centre stone-throwing and glass-breaking continued; at last the mayor positioned himself beneath a lamp near Carfax at about ten o'clock and read the Riot Act. About eleven-thirty the full strength of the special constables was employed to force the crowds away from Carfax and down St Aldates, Cornmarket, Queen Street and High Street. The magistrates were in evidence on the streets until the Tuesday morning. At three that afternoon, the following placard was circulated throughout the city:

> CITY OF OXFORD: - NOTICE, that after one hour from the time proclamation has been made under the Riot Act, all persons remaining or assembling in the streets are guilty of felony. And all householders are earnestly entreated to keep themselves and their families at home after dark, in order that the Magistrates and Police Force may distinguish between orderly citizens and disorderly persons.
>
> JOHN RICHARD CARR Mayor.
>
> P.S. The special constables are requested to be in attendance at the Town Hall at six o'clock punctually.

The chief grievance stated by the rioters was that while colleges and other public establishments were supplied with the best four-pound loaf at seven-pence-halfpenny, the public were forced to pay nine-pence. The outcome was that the mayor, having conferred with leading bakers, agreed to lower the price of the quarter loaf by a penny, an announcement that was met with cheers. On the Tuesday morning, however, Grubb received a note threatening to burn his house to the ground if the reduction was not put into effect within three days. In addition, the Balliol workers' grievances were resolved and the men went back to their jobs. The Guards left Oxford on the Wednesday as they had been ordered to return immediately and they packed up and went in under an hour. This rioting was covered by other provincial newspapers and even made the nationals.

In 1871, *Jackson's* of 16 November assured its readers that Guy Fawkes' rows were now a thing of the past: 'Thanks to good sense on both sides. It had been gradually dwindling down for the last few years, and on Monday last it had totally disappeared, unlike at Cambridge where three undergraduates had been fined for assaulting the police, and three sent for trial at the quarter sessions.'

However, in 1885 Oxford suffered a Guy Fawkes eruption, as reported in *Jackson's*:

> 'The celebration of Guy Fawkes' Day was marked in this city by the appearance of a number of "guys", and in the

evening there was more disorder than has been the case for some years past. Fireworks were discharged and there were several fights between the Undergraduates and the lower class of townspeople, the former using heavy sticks very freely. The University portion of the disorderly crowd were mostly Freshmen, of whom no less than 17 were taken to the police station, while 10 persons belonging to the town shared the same fate. Two cases were brought before the magistrates at the Court on Friday, and the Undergraduates, whose names were taken by the Proctors, will be duly punished.'

In May 1898, when Oxford's new town hall was opened by the Prince of Wales, as expected the undergraduate population attended in force. The Metropolitan Police sent a mounted detachment which was when the trouble started. Instead of recognizing the youngsters' high spirits for what they undoubtedly were, they were seen as a threatening mob. Londoners began to panic and thrash about with their batons so that a number of students were badly beaten and others were ridden down by the police horses. The crowd retaliated and managed to pull a policeman from his horse and trample him underfoot. The students then moved into Cornmarket, down the High Street and into Bear Lane where they met up with the local police, batons at the ready, who drove them out of the lane.

Among this crowd was a well-known Oxford character, F.E. Smith, first Lord Birkenhead and Fellow of Wadham. Caught up in the crowd, he noticed that his college servant was being roughly handled by the police. Smith rushed to help him and was himself arrested and sent to the cells for the night charged with obstructing the police in the lawful execution of their duty. Smith's cell was a brand new one in the recently opened wing of the police courts. As he was shown into it, he raised his hand for silence and said, 'I have great pleasure in declaring this cell open.' With this, he walked inside and slammed the door behind him. At the court hearing he was found not guilty.

Chapter 6

Murder

The medieval examples that follow are taken from the 1285 eyre, a circuit court held in medieval England by a judge (a justice in eyre) who rode from county to county. The hue was a loud shout calling for the chase and capture of a criminal. During this period, residents had to raise the hue in which a crime had committed or else they would be liable to a fine.

Philip de Hybernia stabbed Peter de Virby with a knife in the back, to his heart, so that he died four days later. Philip at once sought sanctuary in St Aldate's church, confessed what he had done, and abjured the realm in front of the coroner. He had no possessions, but lived in the Southwest Ward, and because this took place in daylight and the residents of the parish of St Aldate's failed to capture him, they were to be fined.

Philip of Wales, a clerk from Carmarthen, killed another clerk, William Charles in the suburb of North Osney and as he ran off, was found guilty. The hue was raised but the residents of North Osney did not give chase and so were fined. Afterwards twelve jurors testified that Philip had later returned to Oxford and been captured but had then died in prison.

Richard, squire to Master Thomas de Luda, was killed on the great bridge of Oxford, that is Grandpont, by Hugh of Ireland and Master John de Thorney. Hugh and John fled at once and were believed guilty; they were therefore outlawed. Nothing was known of their possessions, because they were clerks from Ireland. Because the townspeople failed to capture them, even though the murder took place during the hours of daylight, they were fined.

James de Hybernia, clerk, killed William de Burford outside the Smith Gate, and was arrested and imprisoned in the Oxford town prison, where he died. The first finder had died. No-one else was suspected of the killing. The parish of St Peter in the East failed to come to the inquisition; therefore it was to be fined.

Robert de Sunningwell was arrested for the death of Richard of Wales and imprisoned in Oxford Castle, in the custody of Thomas de Sancto Vigore, who was then sheriff. He escaped from Thomas's custody and Thomas was therefore subject to judgement for the escape. Robert immediately took sanctuary in St George's church in the castle, confessed his deed, and abjured the realm before the coroner. He had no chattels, nor was he in any town ward.

John de Candene was arrested for the death of the parson of Easton and imprisoned in Oxford Castle, in the custody of William de Insula, a former sheriff who had since died. He escaped from prison and therefore William's son and heir, Roger de Insula, was subject to judgement. John immediately took sanctuary in the church of St Peter in the East, confessed to killing the parson, and abjured the realm before the coroner. He had no possessions, nor was he in any ward, because he was an outsider. Afterwards Roger came and said that the escape happened in the time of his father William, and asked whether he ought to be responsible for the escape but he was declared subject to judgement.

The first inquest listed on the Coroner's Roll of John of Osney covering the years 1297-1301, was held on 4 February 1296/7. One John Metescarp, a citizen of Oxford had been found dead in the St Aldate's house of medical man, Ralph the Surgeon. Metescarp had been wounded with an arrow and Michael, manciple of Bole Hall, in St Peter in the East parish, was accused of his murder.

Next, on 7 March 1296/7, came the inquest of William de Neusham, John de Lytegrene's servant, who died in St Martin's. He and John's other servants had seen John Beneyt junior pissing between two stalls. Drawing his sword, Neusham struck John, who ran to his father's house. Both Beneyts came out with John de Walteford, and in the consequent brawl William was killed by John junior. The coroner found that he had a wound on the front of his head six inches long and four wide.

On 20 January 1298 Thomas Yve found sawyer Robert de la Marche dead outside a house near the North Gate and immediately raised the hue. Around twilight the previous evening de la Marche had ventured outside the North Gate where he encountered four Irish clerks, probably students. For reasons that are not explained, one of them stabbed him under his left arm. The attacker fled but the other three Irishmen were later arrested.

William de Heyworth of Holywell died after being struck on the head with a hatchet by a neighbour named Reginald le Messer, a poor resident of the Hospital of St John. On 17 June 1298 the coroner learnt that Reginald had run away and could not be found.

Under 1 March 1298, a clerk named Fulco Neyrmyt died in his lodgings in St Mildred's parish. At the inquest it was found that he had a wound on his left eye and his brain had been pierced by a small arrow that almost went through his whole head. The jury, composed as was usual of men from the surrounding parishes, deposed that Fulco, with a gang of other students, had come into the High Street between the churches of All Saints and St Mary the Virgin, just after nine at night. They were armed with bows and arrows, swords and buckers, slings and stones and attacked any townsmen that they came across, badly wounding them. They then broke into the shops and houses of certain townspeople and took away their belongings. Not surprisingly there was a great uproar and the citizens came out to retaliate. When Fulco had used up all his arrows, he came to the home of Edward and Basilia de Erkalewe, just by the church of St Mary the Virgin where, protected by his shield, he attacked the premises and urged his companions to do the same and plunder the couple's belongings. At this, Edward went to an upper window to defend his property with his own bow and arrow and when Fulco peered over the edge of his shield, Edward shot him in the left eye. He died of his wounds, having had the last rites.

Foolish Margery of Hereford who died in a house in St Aldates, after one Richard (surname unknown) had gone to bed one evening with her. When she asked for her fee, he drew a knife and then stabbed her by her left breast one inch wide and five inches deep. She did live long enough to receive the last rites. The inquest held on 26 April 1299 stated that around the hour of curfew, a clerk whom the jurors did not know, 'led Margery to the King's Hall' and she had sex with him there. Richard had immediately run away and could not be arrested because he had not been found.

Under 17 August 1300, Gervase Maddak, a Welsh youth, was found dead in St Edward's Hall. The jury found that he had finally succumbed to a wound received back in February, when he had been struck on the head by a cudgel wielded by Robert le Porter of Winchenden while visiting an inn. The culprit had fled – where no-one knew – leaving behind his cudgel.

John de Ripon was found dead in St Michael at the Northgate. The coroner heard on 18 December 1300 that he had been arguing with

Richard de Maltby also from Yorkshire, during which Richard hit John on the head and John died instantly. Richard had fled and was not to be found.

On 22 December 1300, the coroner sat on Henry de Bokyngham, found dead in St Mary the Virgin parish, with one wound in his skull apparently made by a hatchet and another beneath his left eye, thought to be a knife wound. He had gone to the crossroads called la Wytecrouch [Whitecross, near Abingdon], on his way to Oxford, and had been killed by unidentified robbers.

On 21 August 1306, around midday, Gilbert de Foxlee, clerk, died in his lodgings in the parish of St Peter in the East, Oxford. The following day he was examined by Thomas Lisewys, the king's coroner of the town of Oxford, and found to have a wound in his left shin, below the knee, four inches in diameter and one and a half inches deep. An inquest was thereupon held before the coroner; the jurors said under oath that on the evening of the festival of the Nativity of St John Baptist [23 June] previous, the tailors of Oxford and other townsmen who were with them, spent the whole night in their shops, singing and entertaining themselves with harps, viols and various other instruments, as is their practice and the custom there and elsewhere regarding the celebration of that festival. After midnight, when they did not expect anyone to be wandering in the streets, they and the others who were with them left the shops and took their choir out into the High Street heading for the drapery. As they were enjoying themselves, they suddenly came upon Gilbert de Foxlee with his sword drawn and naked in his hand. He immediately started to argue with them, demanding to join their choir. Since they had among their number some persons of note, they approached him and asked him to go away and not cause anyone any trouble. Gilbert was not prepared to agree to this, but broke away from them and then dogged their footsteps, hurling insults at a certain William de Cleydon and threatening to cut off his hand with his sword unless William promptly surrendered to him his place in the choir. At this, Henry de Beaumont, a returned crusader, Thomas de Bloxham, William de Leye, a servant, John de Leye, and William de Cleydon rushed at Gilbert. Henry wounded him on the right arm with his sword, Thomas stabbed him in the back with a dagger, while William de Cleydon felled him with a blow to the head. Immediately after, William de Leye used a type of battle-axe to give Gilbert the wound on his left leg, by the knee, from which he died on 21 August, having lived for eight weeks and two and a half days and having received the last rites.

On 7 December 1301, Hugh Russel, a Welsh clerk, succumbed in his lodgings to a lung-piercing wound he had received four days previously, as a result of an argument in which he had become involved with another Welshman, Master Elias de Montgomery. After wounding Hugh with a knife, Elias had fled.

Under 9 December 1301, John de Hampslape, a clerk from Northamptonshire, was found dead in Cat Street with a knife wound to the heart, William le Schovelere who discovered him, having raised hue. The jury determined that on the previous day around the hour of curfew John had come out of the room where he lodged, on the north side of 'the great school', in order to urinate, when he heard an argument underway between two fellow clerks who lodged in a room on the south side of the school. Upon investigating, John saw one of the clerks, Nicholas de la Marche, draw a knife with the intention of attacking the other clerk, Thomas of Horncastle. John thrust himself between the two to try to prevent violence, only to receive the blow intended for Thomas. Because this happened at night, no hue was raised at that time, and Nicholas was able to make his escape.

On 3 December 1679:

'One Mr John White (student in Balliol College) was most barbarously butchered by a cursed villain, who, understanding that the Student had money, broke open his door and trunk and took away his money and together with it some linen, but in the meantime the Student came up and caught him in the fact, then the rogue being betrayed. Most cruelly and inhumanely knocked down the said Scholar with a hatchet which he had in his hand, cut a piece off his chin, beat his nose flat, cut one of his ears in two places, and brake his skull in several places and having most wonderfully abused the body of the deceased, made his escape.

'The next day the body was found weltering in its gore, whereupon present enquiry was made. "When had he been seen?" Answer was returned "Not since the evening of the day before," at which time the murderer was seen to go towards his chamber. Then diligent search was made for this fellow; he was found and apprehended who had in his custody above 20 pounds of the murdered person's money, with a shirt of his on his back and upon strict examination confessed the whole fact.'

The ghost of Mary Blandy is said to haunt the castle area. On 6 April 1752 she was hanged there for poisoning her father, Francis, over several months with powdered arsenic that she gave him in gruel. She claimed that she believed that it was a love potion that would endear her aristocratic but already married suitor, William Cranstoun, to her disapproving parent. The trial took place in the Divinity School on 3 March and was notable for its early use of forensic evidence. The case and subsequent execution attracted a great deal of attention, generating pamphlets and press coverage. Miss Blandy, while fettered, hosted tea parties in her quarters in the castle and on her last day alive requested that she be not hanged too high, for decency's sake. Once dead, she was cut down and as there was no coffin or other suitable container at hand, her corpse was carried through the streets over a man's shoulder like a side of meat. She was buried in the parish church at Henley where the poisoning took place but the site is now unknown.

In May 1754, just before an important local election, a Whig procession was going along the High Street in Oxford when a sweep's boy named Joseph Holloway was shot on Magdalen Bridge. He died on 1 June in spite of treatment by a surgeon named Glass. The inquest's verdict which was given the next day stated 'wilful murder by person in a post-chaise drawn by grey horses.' This person was identified as a Captain Turton. At the Assizes on Wednesday, 24 July Turton was tried for the murder but was found not guilty. There have been curious repercussions from the killer being allowed to go free. A ghostly tale relates how a man was returning home over Magdalen Bridge when, in the mist, he saw a dark shape that seemed to topple over the bridge into the river beneath. He told the police what he had seen, but they were not particularly worried, as they had had many reports of a 'black man' falling off the bridge. They had even dragged the river on several occasions, but nothing had ever been found.

The Brasenose College website (www.bnc.ox.ac.uk) under 'a Brasenose scandal' relates how, at about eleven-thirty on the night of

6 December 1827, two young women went to the windows of the rooms of a student of that college. One of them, 24-year-old Ann Priest, who came from Hereford, was known in Oxford as Ann Crutchley or Crotchley. The other girl, whom she had only met a couple of days previously was a Harriet Mitchell and both seem to have been prostitutes.

The rooms in question must have been in either Brasenose Lane or Radcliffe Square as they were the only sets allocated to undergraduates at the time and may now form part of the Lodge and President's Lodgings. The name of the occupant has not been recorded but he must have been having a party when the girls arrived as seven or eight young men came to the window. Ann asked for some wine but as there was none a third-year undergraduate, Houstonne John Radcliffe, offered her brandy instead. When she accepted, he passed out a teapot filled with brandy which both girls drank; it was later estimated that Ann might have drunk up to a pint. Nothing more seemed to come of the incident and eventually the party dispersed, Radcliffe going off to his rooms near the chapel in what is now New Quad.

Ann and Harriet appear to have parted company after leaving Brasenose as Harriet later collapsed in New Inn Hall Street and Ann in Blue Boar Lane, both dead drunk. Ann was seen in this condition by the night-watchman who was later to return and find her bleeding. She was carried off to her lodgings where she was attended by a doctor at eight o'clock the next morning, and again that evening; she died the next morning. A post mortem showed that she had died from internal wounds that *Jackson's* declined to describe 'from motives of decency'. The coroner's jury returned a verdict of murder and both city and the university offered rewards of £100 for information leading to the conviction of the murderer. In the event, nobody was tried for it and only one person was shown to have been alone with her and there was insufficient evidence to bring about a conviction.

On 15 December 1827, the £100 reward for Ann Crutchley's murder was posted:

£100 Reward

CITY OF OXFORD

At a MEETING of the MAGISTRATES, holden This Day
it appeared that a Coroner's Inquest was taken yesterday

in the parish of St Thomas, on view of the body of ANN CROTCHLEY, a young woman who died on Saturday last, at her lodgings, whither she was conveyed by some Watchmen at an early hour on Friday morning, from a passage in Blue Boar Lane, being found there apparently in a state of intoxication, and bleeding profusely. The Jury found a verdict of Wilful Murder by some Person or Persons unknown; and it appearing upon the testimony of two Surgeons, that the death was occasioned by a wound inflicted with a sharp instrument on the body of the deceased, a reward of ONE HUNDRED POUNDS is hereby offered to any person who will give such information as shall lead to the discovery and conviction of the atrocious offender or offenders, to be paid by the Treasurer of the City of Oxford.

JOHN HICKMAN, Mayor
Oxford, Dec. 11th, 1827.

The gruesome sequel was the exhumation of Ann's body for further examination about a fortnight after her death. Six doctors were unanimous that she had died of injuries inflicted with a sharp stick. Contemporary newspaper reports indicate a suspicion that a rumour concerning depraved students was doing the rounds, which provoked the university into insisting on the exhumation in order to prove that her death was not caused by the brandy given to her at Brasenose.

Coincidence or not, the college's records indicate that Radcliffe left Brasenose either late on the night of Ann's death or early the next morning and did not come back into residence the following term. At a college meeting on 31 January 1828, the following was entered into the minutes: 'HJ Radcliffe, having admitted that he gave to Ann Crutchely [*sic*] on the evening of 5th December last intoxicating liquor from one of the Windows of this College; Resolved that being now absent he be not allowed to return till after the Long Vacation.' However, Radcliffe never did return to Brasenose. His name remained on the books as a member of the college until 19 October 1829, when notice was received of his death, less than two years after he left Oxford.

From 11 November 1871: when it was announced that early that morning a shocking murder had been discovered a ripple of horrified excitement ran through the city. The place where it had taken place, a field adjoining the main Botley turnpike road and Binsey Lane, was visited by thousands of people. The victim was a 33-year-old woman named Betsy Richards who had been living with an elderly man called Hopkins in Wyatt's Yard off High Street, St Thomas's. She was described as being of loose habits and made a precarious living by selling matches, hence her nickname of 'Matchy'. She was often to be seen near the Great Western Railway Station and it was established that she had been seen walking near the turnpike gate early on a Sunday morning; it was a not uncommon occurrence for she was in the habit of wandering about at night. The inquest heard how she was of weak intellect and subject to fits. About seven that morning she was found in the field by a labourer called William Flexon, her head half-severed from her body, and quite dead.

Flexon informed the police and the body was removed to the Holly Bush Inn, Osney. It was stated that the body had been moved some eighteen yards as a trail of blood was found between the corpse and a great pool of gore. Medical opinion was that she would not have been able to cry for help as she could not speak. The cut was deep and somewhat jagged and ran from the front of the throat in a slanting direction to just below the right ear, severing both the jugular vein and carotid artery. Suicide was ruled out, partly because of the position of the wound and also because of the fact that no knife was found nearby.

Robbery was not likely to have been a motive as a small leather purse containing four shillings, four-pence and three farthings was still on her person. The only clue to the presence of someone else in the field was the discovery of first the bowl of a pipe containing a small amount of tobacco and later its stem. Later that day, however, a boy came across a large blade near the Holly Bush. It had recently been sharpened and had dark stains that, on later being examined under a microscope proved not to be blood.

Some days later the police were informed that a Botley man had bought a clasp knife in Queen Street the day before the murder but it was proved that he had later sold the knife to somebody else. The river was thoroughly searched for the murder weapon with no success and no clue about the murder was forthcoming despite a reward of £100 for the discovery of the murderer.

From 29 June 1886: Hiram Bowell of Dover's Row, St Clement's attempted a double murder after he had become suspicious of a series of visits which a man named Simmonds paid to his house while Bowell was out at work. One day, after hearing that Simmonds was in the house, Bowell ran back and finding him still there wounded him in the throat with a bread knife. When the knife handle fell out, Simmonds was able to get away but Bowell drew out a pocket knife and attacked his wife, slashing her throat in two places so deeply that he left her for dead. Simmonds followed him as he was leaving the house and called a nearby police sergeant who promptly arrested Bowell. Both stab victims were taken to the Radcliffe Infirmary where his wounds were dressed and hers were stitched up and proved not to be fatal although they bled freely. Simmonds stated that he had indeed been to the Bowells' home several times to meet another man who had not been there on the occasion in question. He had been sitting quietly eating bread and cheese with Mrs Bowell's sister and brother-in-law when Bowell burst into the house and set about him for no apparent reason.

Chapter 7

Immorality

Sexual misdemeanours usually resulted in recriminations against offenders. These could be imposed by the law, by society, or both. Every edition of *Jackson's* carries reports of women appearing in court for immoral activities and many had previous convictions. Even if the current offence was not connected with morality, those of dubious reputation had this fact mentioned. Much of this behaviour was antisocial, being drunk and disorderly, using foul language, behaving in a riotous manner, or simply idling, presumably with intent, in short being a public nuisance.

In 1443 a prostitute named Lucy Colbrand was solemnly banished from the precincts of the university for her 'numerous crimes and their consequences'. As was normal, the banishment took the form of a long formula in Latin. Another banishment is recorded ten years later, on 16 June 1453, when Margaret Curtoys was placed in the pillory for persistent prostitution and when released was banished from Oxford forever.

In the chancellor's court on 28 June 1452 Robert Smyth, alias Harpmaker, from the Canditch (today's Broad Street), was accused of adultery with Joan FitzJohn who lived at the end of Catte Street, near St Mary's church. Joan is described as 'a wandering barmaid'. Robert was ordered to abjure, that is formally renounce, her company and to avoid anywhere that she was likely to be whether it was the public street, market, church or chapel, under pain of a fine of forty shillings for contravening the authority of the university.

In September 1458 Thomas Bentlee, alias Deneley, 'organpleyer' at All Souls College appeared to answer the charge that he had been discovered alone in a chamber with a woman in St Peter in the East parish. She was the wife of John Gwasmere, a cook at Merton College, and the pair had committed the offence about noon on 4 September, the feast of St Cuthbert. Bentley was sent to prison but released, repentant and in tears, after only three hours thanks to the intervention of the warden of

All Souls who gave him a good character reference and vouched for his future conduct.

On 11 August 1466, the widow of Philip Marcham was forbidden to entertain scholars at her house. It was, the court heard, 'the constant resort of immoral and turbulent scholars and [she was] suspected of other malpractices and forbidden to entertain scholars in future, and to sell beer.' Medieval cases are interesting because they mention guilty males, whereas in later ones the female is blamed.

Later punishments were being sent to the House of Correction, imprisonment with or without hard labour and solitary confinement.

In 1717 John Dry published the poem *Merton Walks or the Oxford Beauties* that describes Sunday night promenades in that college's gardens during the spring and summer when they were 'thronged' with young gentlemen and gentlewomen. However, this seemingly innocent pastime grew so scandalous that the gate to the garden was securely locked so that 'the young gentlemen and others betook themselves to Magdalen College walk' which subsequently was filled every Sunday night during the summer 'just like a fair'.

The city authorities seem to have been well aware of the different degrees of perceived immorality and the descriptions vary accordingly. Some women were referred to by the Victorian euphemism 'unfortunate' while others ranged from being 'a notorious prostitute' to a 'common' one, while other women were 'lewd and disorderly', 'rogues and vagabonds found wandering the streets' and 'using indecent language'. A particularly offensive example reported on 29 November 1874 concerning Eliza Gibbs, a prostitute living in Friars Street, was considered so disgusting that the bench refused it to be repeated in court and 'it was committed to paper' by PC Pancutt, the police officer who had brought the charge. Gibbs was fined ten shillings and sixpence with seven and sixpence costs with the alternative of fourteen days' hard labour. Not long afterwards, in August 1876, Martha Neville of Paradise Street was charged with being a disorderly prostitute in Church Street, St Ebbe's by using obscene language the night before. When asked by Alderman Carr how old she was, she replied that she was 16. PC Parker stated that 'she had been following her present course of life for twelve months.' The bench sent her to prison for fourteen days' hard labour, and hinted that they would find out what could be done to try to get her to mend her ways.

The situation in Oxford, and Cambridge, was unique in that the proctors, the officers in charge of discipline, were allowed to arrest women of bad repute and send them to gaol, even if they were not in the company of members of the university. Letters were sent to national newspapers complaining that when the proctors attempted to remove these nuisances from the streets they were accused of abusing them. The same names appear in court records over and over again for similar offences, some of them local girls, others had come to Oxford in the expectation of earning a better living. When unable to find a respectable position, they sold their wares on the streets and subsequently ended up in prison. With the arrival of trains and the improvement in services the position worsened as women came from as far away as London for a night's work.

After nine o'clock in the evening, only the vice-chancellor and his associates were empowered to stop violence in the town, arrest troublemakers, and deal with prostitution. The university was very much against the city police becoming involved, which did not meet with the approval of the city fathers. This meant that out of Term there was no police supervision after nine o'clock.

The university was in a very testing position, generating censure whatever decision was made as it was seen as either too severe or too lenient. In his *Political Register* of 1814, William Cobbett attacked the university for having authority over those townspeople who were not members or privileged persons and criticized the workings of the vice-chancellor's court.

Although legislation regarding the university's authority included ways in which to deal with antisocial behaviour of all kinds, it is prostitution that attracted the most attention. On 26 February 1825, the vice-chancellor himself informed Home Secretary Sir Robert Peel that the situation was critical as the university had only the two proctors and their four pro-proctors. It had the authority to eject prostitutes but not the manpower to enforce it. The proctors were permitted to arrest, and the vice-chancellor to imprison them as 'lewd, idle & disorderly persons' and to send those with no right to be in Oxford back to their home parishes.

However, under new legislation, they could not be imprisoned unless they behaved in a 'riotous & indecent manner' and could no longer be sent home. This had led to a great increase in both numbers and insubordination and attracted numerous complaints resulting in the now notorious Vagrancy Act of 1824 that allowed the vice-chancellors of both Oxford and Cambridge to appoint constables with normal police powers to act within four miles and apprehend prostitutes under the Universities Act of the following year.

On 16 July 1825, *Jackson's* reported on the University Police Bill. The section concerning prostitutes read:

> 'And be it further enacted, that every common prostitute and night-walker, found wandering in any public walk, street, or high-way, within the precincts of the said University of *Oxford*, and not giving a satisfactory account of herself, shall be deemed an idle and disorderly person, within the true intent and meaning of an Act passed in the last Session of parliament, intituled *an Act for the punishment of idle and disorderly persons, and rogues and vagabonds in that part of* Great Britain *called* England, and shall and may be apprehended and dealt with accordingly.'

So, in May 1849 22-year-old Maria Haines, a common prostitute, was sent to prison for three weeks' hard labour for having conducted herself in a disorderly and indecent way in the city streets the previous day.

In November the next year the town clerk approached the Hebdomadal Board for a contribution towards the cost of maintaining convicted prostitutes in the city gaol. Following the Vagrancy Act, the average daily number of those sent by the university had decreased from nine to less than one. The cost of upkeep was seven-pence-halfpenny a day for healthy women, which was about two-thirds of the prisoners, the rest requiring medical care which added a further daily seven-pence. An offer of ten-pence a day was made.

The *Report of the Governor of the House of Industry* for the previous year appeared in *Jackson's* on 16 July 1836. Much of it related to the effects of the New Poor Law. As regards immoral women, he said that overseers of the poor were:

> 'on the alert and many were found so officious in the discharge of what they considered their duty (through the fear of a child becoming chargeable to their parish) that

frequently females, under the least suspicion, were pursued, and often the most disgusting and revolting enquiries were made, and even character traduced, without foundation; and what was still worse, the old law afforded the abandoned prostitute the means of affixing the fruits of her prostitution upon those whom she thought she could make the greatest advantage of; and he trusted he should be excused by repeating that the enormous sum of £1500 has been paid by the rate-payers of Oxford in support of illegitimate children, as the books of the house [of Industry] would fully show, and nearly the whole of which may be considered as debt irrecoverably lost; and he had no hesitation in further stating that a considerable portion of the money had been paid in aid of prostitution, since it appears by those books that some of the mothers have had two and even three bastards, subsisting either on parish relief or on the funds of the putative father, when the money could be obtained from him.'

In a letter to the editor of the *Oxford Journal* dated 29 January 1842, sheriff James Hunt wrote about conditions for prostitutes held in the city gaol. 'It is true that I have repeatedly noticed and mentioned the want of better cells for those unfortunate persons, and have constantly deplored the absence of proper endeavours to reform and reclaim the unhappy victims of prostitutions, some of whom are often imprisoned for periods of different duration three or four times in a year.' Writing further on about the practice of putting prisoners in solitary confinement: 'If that form of punishment (which undoubtedly the severest and most distressing to be borne) is to be continued, not only our own gaol but any other in the kingdom will require the alterations so humanely and judiciously directed by the Home Secretary.'

The History of the University of Oxford: Nineteenth-century Oxford, edited by M.G. Brock and M.C. Curthoys, includes several entries concerning prostitution. Quoting the *Oxford Protestant Magazine*, I (May 1847) 111, it writes that the estimated number of women on the streets at night could be as many as 100 out of a total population of between 300 and 500 (p. 280). *The History,* p. 281, points out that prostitution affected attitudes to students being allowed to lodge outside of colleges; Dr Pusey in particular being very much against this as he seemed to think that 'sleeping in' would prevent vice.

Jackson's recorded that on 7 December 1867, the sheriff told the city court that he had been approached by one of the prisoners in the city gaol who claimed that 'she had been most improperly walked off by one of the University police, while arm-in-arm with a commercial traveller in the High-street.' The mayor replied that he would contact the proctors about it.

An article in *Jackson's* of 4 November 1893, covers a meeting convened to discuss the possible abolition of St Giles's Fair, or else the introduction of greatly increased police supervision during the two days that it was held. The Vicar of St Giles's church pointed out that drunkenness and 'indiscriminate kissing' had a detrimental effect on morals as at least one servant girl had been 'ruined' by attending – and with the fleshpots of Jericho just round the corner! In addition, it made the working classes 'improvident'. The fair was said to be an anachronism that should be allowed to fade into history as similar events had done. Interestingly, no mention is made of possible accidents, indeed fatalities. In the event, of course no such closure took place, thanks to the weight of tradition combined with vested interests.

Apart from venereal disease, the most unwelcome outcome of immorality was illegitimate children. Oxford parishes have the normal collection of bastardy bonds going back to the sixteenth century but two entries in a college baptism register are most unusual. These are for illegitimate children of Charles II. One was George Fitzroy, a natural son of the king born in Merton College in December 1665 by Barbara Palmer, and the second was another bastard son born in February 1668.

The fate of the vast majority of children born out of wedlock was nowhere near as happy as these royal children. For example, from *Jackson's* 16 September 1784:

'between 9 and 10 p.m., found a male child only a few days old – in passage of the Jolly Trooper pub, at corner of Bear Lane, Oxford. It had on a clean shirt and cap and was wrapped in old flannel. A notice was issued about the child: "Left between 9 and 10 p.m. at door of Mr Charles McDonald, parish of All Saints, Oxford – a male child c.10 days old. Reward – 2 guineas from Treasurer of the Incorporated

Parishes within City of Oxford, for information leading to apprehension of person who left child or about person to whom child belongs."'

Even less fortunate were the following women. Hannah Fletcher, a single woman who appeared before the city court in January 1830 in order to ascertain the father of her bastard child. In the course of her being examined it came out that this was her third illegitimate child, each by a different man; these, she admitted, she had only met once in the street. The magistrates, by order of the governor of the Board of Guardians, committed her to the city gaol for three calendar months as a lewd woman.

From 11 February 1832: Thomas Hawkins appeared before the city court to answer a charge of bastardy made by Betty Cripps who had sworn before magistrates that she had recently given birth to a female child and that Hawkins was the father. He was ordered to pay two shillings but as he was unable to do so was sent to the city gaol for three months. However, Betty Cripps admitted that this was the fourth illegitimate child for whom she had named a father so the magistrates made an example of her and sent her to prison as a lewd woman for twelve calendar months.

From 25 October 1834: Mary Ann Hill, a young woman who had recently given birth to a bastard child in the House of Industry, was committed to the House of Correction for two calendar months as a lewd woman. The reason that made the Board of Guardians apply to the magistrates for a committal was the gross perjury committed by this young woman when she was examined in order to identify the father of the child so that a paternity order could be served on him.

On 22 July 1882, *Jackson's* published the Registrar General's figures for 1880 showing that the rate of illegitimate births in Oxfordshire was 6.4 per cent as opposed to 5.1 per cent countrywide. The distribution of these illegitimate births included sixteen males and fourteen females in Oxford itself and twenty-two males and nineteen females in the adjoining Headington registration district. *Jackson's* comments that, compared with 1879, it was 'a little singular that there was an increase of nine illegitimate boys and a decrease of nine illegitimate girls.'

These were the relatively lucky ones as others never stood a chance. Unfortunately, babies who had been murdered or whose cause of death was suspect were far too common.

The best remembered example of infanticide is that of Anne Greene who was hanged in the castle on 14 December 1649 for killing her bastard child. As was usual for murderers, her body was taken to the Anatomy School to be dissected. The Reader in Anatomy, Dr Petty, noticed that her body was unexpectedly warm and he and his staff managed to bring Anne round. Unsurprisingly she was stunned but after a few days she was able to speak once more. She was quite oblivious of anything that had happened to her after her fetters were removed prior to execution and was never able to remember her dreadful experiences despite having a normal married life with more children.

Some ten years later, something similar took place when Dr Conyers of St John's College took charge of another girl who had been hanged for infanticide. He too managed to revive her only for the bailiffs, led by a certain Henry Mallory, to prevent her from escaping her fate. Just after midnight they broke into the house where she was staying, forced her into a coffin and carted her off to Broken Hayes, now Gloucester Green. Ignoring her cries of 'Lord have mercy on me!' they hanged her from a tree which was later felled by the appalled locals.

On 30 January 1679 Robert Fulk, a former member of Christ Church, got a maid pregnant. As the child was stillborn, he threw it down the college privy house. When this was found out, Fulk was imprisoned in Newgate where he did a lot of good among his fellow prisoners. At the Old Bailey Fulk was condemned to be executed but 'did not die with the rabble, but very privately' at Tyburn at the end of January.

In 1778 a girl named Martha Jewell died in the Radcliffe Infirmary. When going through her belongs, the hospital staff came across the body of a baby girl in a box under the bed. It had been born some eleven days previously. Martha had given birth on her own behind the bed curtains and nobody had noticed an unusually unpleasant smell in the ward.

On 19 June 1784 *Jackson's* reported that Hannah Morris was committed to the castle by Edward Witts, Esq., charged 'with a violent suspicion of murdering her male bastard child, of which she was delivered on 15 or 16 April, on the oaths of Elizabeth Mayow, Ann Wyton and Sarah Prophet.' In another edition, however, it was stated that the child was a girl.

From 6 June 1857: two children, Eleanor Bertha Clark aged 3 ½ and Frances Moreton, aged 5 months, in the care of a Mrs Davison who kept a brothel in Jericho 'met with their deaths in a very mysterious manner', one being burnt to death, the other being suffocated. An inquest, that lasted four hours, was held on their bodies at the Saddlers' Arms in Wellington Street, Jericho. It was stated that Mrs Davison, who was looking after the children for other people who were away from Oxford, had put them to bed about seven-thirty on the evening of their deaths and went out about half an hour later. She returned at ten-fifteen and two other women who lived in the house, came in soon afterwards and they all ate together. About eleven-thirty when all went up to bed they smelt burning. On opening the children's bedroom, they found it full of smoke and the bedding on fire. There was no candle in the room, but there had been matches and Eleanor Clark must have played with them. The elder girl, who had been badly burnt, was already dead and the younger so badly affected that she died the next morning from suffocation, despite a surgeon, Mr Godfrey, being sent for who did all that he could to save her.

Both the children were illegitimate and Mrs Davison was being paid to look after them but she had been paid only thirteen shillings for the baby and nothing for the older one for some time. She admitted that she had had eight or nine children to take care of and of these, five had died. She had ten children of her own but only one was still alive. This was the second inquest on four children at her house. The jury returned the verdict that 'the elder child died from being so severely burnt, and that the younger one died from suffocation, but how the fire originated in the bed room there was no evidence to show.' The jury was all of the opinion that Mrs Davison was not a fit person to be entrusted with the care of children.

From 10 August 1861: a great sensation was created by the discovery of the dead body of a newborn female infant in a garden on the corner of the lane between the Woodstock and Banbury roads. It was discovered by a member of the university police, Samuel Loveday, who owned the garden. Pending an inquest, enquiries were made which focused on a young woman called Harriet Walton, who lodged in Westminster Hall Yard, in St Aldate's who had recently been employed by Mrs Buckingham, a laundress in Adelaide Street. She was suspected of being the child's mother but she had run away from her room and was afterwards taken into custody. Mr Godfrey, the surgeon examined the tiny body and was convinced that it had been born alive and had probably died of exposure.

The chief witness was George Lynes, a brick-maker from Summertown, who had been friendly with Harriet Walton and had gone with her the previous Sunday evening to the Wesleyan chapel in

New Inn Hall Street. Afterwards they had walked back together up to Summertown. After a while the girl became so ill that Lynes called on Mrs Eli Gibbs for help. After drinking some water, they started off back to Oxford but she was again taken ill and sat by the side of the footpath. At Harriet's request, Lynes fetched Mrs Buckingham; when they returned they found Harriet crouched up against one of the new houses near St Giles's church, having moved about 100 yards.

Mr Rusher, surgeon at the city gaol said that she appeared to have given birth and the matron at the gaol said that she had confessed that she had done so while Lynes was away fetching Mrs Buckingham. She insisted that Mrs Buckingham knew nothing of this, and that Lynes was definitely the child's father but had not even realized that she was pregnant as she had denied it to both of them. Following the judge's advice, the jury returned a verdict of 'wilful murder' after which she was committed to trial at the next Assizes.

From 3 June 1865: an inquest was held at the Odd Fellows' Arms in George Street on the body of a 'female infant child unknown'. A builder's labourer from New Street, St Ebbe's, named Ambrose Pearce, related how about two o'clock in the morning in question he and another man were employed in emptying the reservoir belonging to two houses in Broken Hayes that his master had recently bought. Pearce did not know who had owned them.

After a couple of hours' work he came across a bundle, made up of an ordinary cotton apron, which was found to contain the dead body of a baby girl. He sent off to the university police station and officers came to investigate.

The body was taken to the public house in the state in which it was viewed by the coroner and jury, although it had become somewhat discoloured. The second labourer, Joseph Prater of Abbey Place, St Ebbe's, corroborated Pearce's evidence. Henry Mallam, surgeon to the Oxford union workhouse, examined the corpse and said that it was full term but could not be sure that it had been born alive although he believed that it had. From the ragged umbilical cord, he guessed that the mother had not received any medical attention and that the child could have been dead a fortnight at most. There was a wound in the throat but due to decomposition he could not say if it was the cause of death. The jury returned the verdict 'Wilful murder against person or persons unknown.'

From 17 June 1871: an 18-year-old servant girl named Mary Ann Sutton, working for Mr E. Turner in Blenheim Place, St Giles, was committed for 'having destroyed her illegitimate offspring in a diabolical manner.' The case created a great sensation in the city.

The girl's mistress, Mrs Turner, stated that the girl had apparently been in good health until a few days previously when she said that she was very poorly and was given some brandy after which she recovered and went back to work. Mrs Turner remarked that she was looking very stout but she insisted that there was nothing wrong with her. After tea, Mrs Turner went up to Mary Ann's room and found her sitting there, her dress unfastened and from what she saw, Mrs Turner sent immediately for the family medical man, Mr Owen, who did not come until gone eleven that evening.

Edward Owen stated that when he went into the girl's room she was in bed and Mrs Turner showed him a chamber pot in which there was a clot of blood. Owen examined the girl internally and was left in no doubt that she had recently given birth but she denied this. Owen told her that he was not to be fooled and started to search the room where he found several napkins saturated with blood and still wet. In the end, Mary Ann confessed that the baby was in the coal yard. It was found under the coal, naked and Owen put it into a bucket and washed it. It was a newborn boy which had gone full term. There were four clean cuts in the flesh on the left side of the neck, one of which was two inches long and very deep although it had failed to divide a main artery. There was a clean cut to the right side of the neck and a superficial cut to the nose. The skull was badly crushed. There proved to be internal injuries that indicated considerable violence. After this examination Owen asked the girl where the afterbirth was and was told that she had burnt it. After a short deliberation the jury returned the verdict of 'Wilful murder'.

From 20 March 1886: at St Stephen's Villa, Abbey Road, Osney, the body of an illegitimate female child belonging to a single woman named Florence Batts was the subject of an inquest. The coroner remarked that the child was newborn and its mother unmarried. He had no doubt that it had died of natural causes but he was sure that the jury would agree that he was right to hold this enquiry.

Adelaide Batts, a widow, stated that the baby was the child of her daughter Florence, a dress-maker and a single woman. Mrs Betts had been a midwife at Queen Charlotte's and King's College hospitals and had attended her daughter herself. The mother was too ill for the child to be brought to her and it did not survive long as it was constitutionally weak. Its mother had been seriously ill ever since the birth. No doctor had been called until she was much worse after two days and Dr Jenkins was sent for. He did not come and Florence recovered only to get worse again when he did attend and now she was in a critical state. The child's birth and death had not been registered.

The coroner remarked to the jury that it was quite clear that the child was born alive. Both the doctor and the registrar 'seemed to be waiting for the mother's death in order to bury the child with her.' Naturally Mrs Bates was anxious to conceal the birth and although her actions had not been criminal it was serious enough to warrant an enquiry. The line, he said, 'between accidentally and intentionally disposing of a body was narrow, and the Registrars were naturally suspicious of these things, hence the enquiry.' The jury returned the verdict 'that the child died from constitutional weakness.'

From 2 June 1888: an inquest was held at the city police station on the body of a male child found dead in the open street. It had not died under suspicious circumstances. The coroner had called an enquiry because it was a 'scandalous thing to expose the body of a child like that in the open daylight.' John Money, a builder of Kingston Road related how he had been walking round affluent Polstead Road on a Sunday morning when at the corner of a pile of bricks he saw a child, all exposed to the air, perfectly naked. He saw that it was dead, and so informed a policeman who put it in a basket and took it away. Mr Ballard, a surgeon, said that there were no signs of violence and thought that the child had never breathed and was therefore still-born. A verdict of 'still-born' was returned accordingly.

From 7 June 1890: an inquest was held in the Settling Room in the cattle market, Gloucester Green, on an unidentified male infant discovered in the Thames near Osney Lock the previous evening. The coroner found that it was a child, not a newborn but probably two or three weeks old. There was no indication of the identity of the mother or where it had come from. Due to the advanced state of decomposition it was impossible to establish the cause of death and whether or not it was from natural causes. On being exposed to the little corpse, 'the smell from which was so horrible that they [the jury] made a speedy exit.' When the body was opened up an examination revealed that the child had not been still-born, that it had been fed milk and 'there were some faeces on a napkin'. It was stated that the baby might have been dead a week or in the water for at least four days. There were some signs of smothering but nothing conclusive. The jury returned an open verdict to allow for any possible future findings.

From 8 April 1893: an inquest held at the Plough Inn, Wolvercote heard how the body of a newborn male child had been found in a culvert running under the Woodstock Road by a retriever dog that had brought the naked body out of the culvert in its mouth. There was a very strong suspicion that the infant had been murdered.

Medical opinion was that it had been born alive but there were no marks of injury on the body or other indications of the cause of death, neither was there anything to suggest that it had been ill-treated and, although it may have died from natural causes such as convulsions or similar, it was more likely that it had bled to death due to incorrect severing of the umbilical cord. There were no signs of anyone having been in the vicinity of the culvert recently. Enquiries were made at the workhouses and lodging houses in the area and nobody had heard about a recent confinement. The road 'was pestered with tramps just now very much and some who had been noticed in the locality had been traced, but no clue could be ascertained as to the parent.' Enquiries were to continue but in the meantime the jury concluded 'that the child had died from want of proper attention at its birth.'

Chapter 8

Male Sex-Offenders

Being a member of the clergy did not prevent medieval clerics from being sex pests. On 27 July 1444 a priest by the name of Master Hugh Sadler had to swear on the Bible that in future he would abstain from violence, pandering and fornication.

On December 1666 Wood noted that most decent men would agree that there were a number of things that needed to be reformed and had 'crept in among us' since 1660. Bawdy houses and light hussies were giving young men the pox so the disease was very frequent among them, and some suspected pox doctors made a living by it. 'And whereas it was notorious formerly to those that had it, it is now soe common (especially in Exeter College, Xt. Ch., [Christ Church] and...) that they glory of it.' Wood continued: 'Corrupters of youth, such that live obscurely and lurke in the towne taking all advantages to make pray of scollers'. And a year later he wrote: 'An age given over to all vice – whores and harlots, pimps and panders, bauds and buffoons, lechery and treachery, atheists and papists, rogues and rascals, reason and treason, playmakers and stage-players, officers debauched and corrupters (proctor Thomas infected with the pox while proctor) – aggravated and promoted by presbytery.'

Thomas Hearne had a great deal to say about Robert Shippen, the Principal of Brasenose 1710-1745, none of it to his credit. His sins were noted with a good deal of malevolence, branding him as 'a most lecherous man' as well as 'a strange lover of women'. This lecher would pay illicit visits to the wife of a fellow head of house, the President of Trinity, and not content with her attentions, he 'debauched a very pretty Woman, one Mrs. Churchill, the wife and afterwards the widow of one Churchill, a bookbinder in Oxford, one of the prettiest Women in England. He poxed her, of which she died in a sad Condition. The thing is so notorious that 'tis frequently talked of to this day.'

From 21 October 1826: at the city sessions Robert Rouse, a former ostler at the Wheatsheaf Inn in St Aldates, was charged with assaulting Mary Ann White and Esther Burren, girls of about 12 years of age with intent to commit rape. He was found guilty and sentenced to two years' imprisonment, with twelve months for each offence. He was a married man with several children and *Jackson's* understood that his wife was 'a very industrious woman and bears an irreproachable character.'

One Sunday morning in February 1834, during Divine Service, William Higgs, who had been let out of prison that very morning, was picked up by two of the city constables 'in a state of beastly drunkenness, near St Giles's church, and indecently exposing his person.' When the constables went up to him he became very violent and knocked them about; with great difficulty they succeeded in getting him into a barrow and bringing him in. The following day he was committed to the city gaol for hard labour for three calendar months. 'The only reward the constables got for preventing such disgusting scenes from taking place with impunity was a roll in the mud and their clothes torn!'

From 30 April 1836: at the city court Samuel Petty, alias Duncan Petty, was examined after being charged with 'decoying a child, of the name of Maria Freeman, into the fields, and afterwards attempting to strip off her clothes. When she started to shriek loudly he dragged her to the river, near Rewley, and threw her into it then ran away.' Luckily Robert Newman heard her screams and ran up and rescued her from the water. At the same session, another similar charge was brought against Petty which had taken place some six weeks before. He was remanded for further examination.

In October 1884 a labourer named John Baggot was charged with attempting to rape 5-year-old Alice Brain. The court heard how the prisoner had met the little girl at Binsey and enticed her into a field, where he committed the assault of which he was accused. He was found guilty of indecent assault and sentenced to eighteen months' imprisonment with hard labour, all the time protesting his innocence.

Baggot of Union Street, Jericho was later summoned in March 1887 with committing an indecent assault on a child of 6 named Emily Harris of Castle Street. Baggot did not appear in court and the girl's mother stated the facts as she believed them. He handed the magistrates a letter from a medical man who had attended the child. A warrant was issued for the arrest of the accused.

The court was crowded to capacity in June 1856 when it became known that a man dressed as a female was to appear not only for cross-dressing but also for being drunk and incapable of taking care of himself. He had been picked up drunk and asleep near Magdalen College School instead of being in his lodgings in the Flying Horse.

At the university police station he was charged with being a man in disguise. He strongly denied this and allowed the matron to conduct a body search, after which she was satisfied 'that the defendant was not one of her own sex.' He eventually admitted being 'plain Daniel Judge from Birmingham' and that he had worked as a female servant with a French family for two years in London. Judge was found to have upon him a pair of women's pockets containing six shilling, seven-pence-halfpenny, a looking glass, a razor and some rouge.

He appeared in court wearing a straw bonnet trimmed with a coloured ribbon, and a striped dress with flounces, with a light shawl and black veil, with black laced boots and 'altogether was not a bad representative of the opposite sex.' He then stated that his name was Joseph Walker and he had lived as a male waiter at the Eagle in St James Street, London but persuaded to dress as a woman to please two men who took him to Birmingham. He had come to Oxford on his way back to London.

The magistrates did not believe this explanation and put him on remand pending further enquiries. *Jackson's* reported that since the case, a bundle had been found on Headington Hill containing two petticoats, other female clothing and two sets of false hair which the accused admitted to owning.

Edward Padbury, a tailor from George Street, was charged in July 1869 with threatening to kill his wife Mary. The case had already been heard and the prisoner on remand. Alderman Carr described the case as the most heartless and cruel that he had ever heard. Padbury had taken to drinking to excess and brought home prostitutes every night, to the annoyance of his family and the neighbours. Not only had he threatened to kill his wife, whom he had already badly injured, but also horrified and disgusted the neighbourhood where he lived by his offensive language and behaviour. It was stated that the public in general and his wife in particular had to be protected from this man. He was ordered to be locked up until he could provide two sureties of £50 each and to enter into his own recognizance for £100 to keep the peace towards his wife for twelve months. Padbury had seven sovereigns on his person when taken to prison and with his permission the prison governor handed two of them to Mrs Padbury.

George Corfield, a tramp, was charged in September 1875 with indecently exposing himself to a female in Museum Terrace at twenty to eight in the evening the previous month. Evidence was given by Mrs Sophia Tybbits of Museum Terrace and her son, and Corfield was sentenced to three months' hard labour. The chairman remarked that he was sorry that the bench did not have the power to give him twenty lashes and that he was a disgrace to society.

In October 1875 Edward Cue, an Irishman employed on the draining works, was charged with being drunk and indecently exposing himself in the High Street one Saturday afternoon. Evidence was given by William Preston of Blackfriars Road and Cue was sentenced to two months' hard labour.

From 14 August 1886: Alfred Clark, of Cousins's lodging house, St Thomas's was summoned for indecent exposures at Osney Lock. He was also charged, together with William Couling of the Plasterer's Arms Yard, St Thomas's with assaulting Henry Basson, the lock-keeper at the same time.

In April 1887 John Coster, a shoemaker of Church Place, St Ebbe's, was charged with behaving in an indecent, lewd and obscene way in Holywell at nine in the evening towards two young women. One of them gave evidence of the recent offence and added that a similar one had been committed some eight weeks previously between Broad Street and St John's College. He was also charged with assaulting a lady in Crick Road. Coster had been identified by both women and PC Prior said that they had complained to him so he had arrested him in Castle Street. There had been further complaints of similar behaviour in other places. Despite protesting that he had been elsewhere at the time of the offences and bringing character witnesses, the magistrates agreed that he was guilty of the 'horrible charges which had been made against him, and they could not be passed over without severe punishment.' He was sentenced to three months' hard labour for each indecency offence and two months' hard labour for the assault, the sentences making a total of eight months in all.

Edward Sturrage aged 24, a labourer, was charged in January 1888 with indecently exposing himself at the window of his house in Marlborough Road on two instances in December. The defence pointed out that it was necessary in common law 'to show that the offender had exposed himself to "divers liege subjects of the Queen"' whereas in the first case there had only been one witness. The prosecution responded that it was enough for an exposure to have taken place 'where people could see if they had looked.'

The prisoner's mother contended that her son, who had served in India and Malta as a soldier, suffered from abscesses on the lower part of his body on which he had to apply ointment every morning. The recorder remarked that someone who was used to warm climates was hardly likely to stand in front of an open window in January in Oxford.

The jury retired but was unable to come to a unanimous verdict. The recorder threatened to lock them up until they had done so but he had to be off to Northampton so the only course open to him was to dismiss the charges; 'in the name of the citizens of Oxford, he must say he did not thank them for their services.' The case would have to be adjourned until the next city sessions.

In November 1888 William Henry Speer residing at Lilford Lodge, Banbury Road, who was described on the charge sheet as a 'gentleman', was charged with indecently exposing himself at the plantation in Banbury Road on 20, 25 and 27 October 'with intent to insult certain females'. He was also summoned for committing a similar offence on 26 October with intent to insult another girl. The defence, Mr Acland of the Oxford circuit, applied to have the case heard in camera, but the magistrates said that they could not grant this although all the females and young boys had to leave the court.

A surgeon who had been treating Speer said that he had known him for eighteen years and that he had recently treated him as 'his general constitutional condition was at fault, he was in a state of extreme nervous prostration, the action of the heart was slow, and he was not altogether pleased with the condition of his lungs. One effect of that would be that he would frequently not have control of himself physically.' He continued: 'It was well-known in the medical profession that in certain conditions of nervous prostration there was a desire for natural relief which was absolutely uncontrollable' but he did not know if this were the case with Speer.

On announcing their decision, the bench said that it was obvious that Speer had been careful not to show himself when men were around.

He was convicted of three of the charges and sentenced to six weeks' hard labour for each of them, not concurrently but separately as the public had to be protected from such behaviour. Acland gave notice of an appeal and Speer was bailed on his own recognizance of £1,000 with two sureties for £500 each.

At the Epiphany quarter sessions in January 1889, the appeal case of William Henry Speer before the justices of the Bullingdon Division was heard but it was noted that the notices should have been served on the girls and the clerk to the magistrates who accused Speer rather than the bench. After an almost seven-hour session, with searching and intimidating cross-examination of the girls and evidence from character witnesses, it was decided that the court was not satisfied there was an intention to insult therefore the appeal was allowed. This was greeted with some applause.

John Margetts, an 18-year-old labourer of Hayfield Road was indicted in May 1893 for committing an indecent assault on Rose Pacey aged 9 in Hayfield Road. The girl was the daughter of a stonemason and had complained immediately after the assault. Margetts asked her father to overlook the matter as it would be a lesson to him for life. However, Pacey gave evidence in court.

The recorder said that no force or violence was shown to have taken place and he could not help thinking that it was a case in which a little mercy should be shown. Was there any desire to ruin the young man? He suggested that Margetts should withdraw his plea of not guilty to an indecent assault and plead guilty to one of common assault. This the prisoner did and the recorder told him that he hoped he would never repeat the offence and fined him five shillings.

An old offender, Albert Narroway of London Place, St Clement's, was charged with being drunk and disorderly in St Giles's Fair in September 1893. He was found by Detective Sergeant Prior accosting ladies near the entrance to St John's College; he was very drunk. He then went into a nearby tent and sitting next to a lady made himself so objectionable that she pushed him away. Narroway pleaded that he had been so drunk that he did not know what he was doing. He then said he was sorry, and that he hoped that the bench would be lenient with him. As he had several previous convictions the mayor fined him one pound including costs, or fourteen days' imprisonment. The prisoner asked for time to pay the money but was refused.

In December 1876 Harry Foster, 17, of Park End Place, a clerk at Weaving's brewery, was summoned to show cause why he should not contribute towards the support of the illegitimate male child of Annie Allen of another number in Park End Place. The evidence for the paternity having been presented, a number of letters were read, in one of which Foster had written:

> 'When fishes run upon the earth,
> And fire begins to freeze,
> That is the time my love for you will cease.'

Loud laughter in the courtroom. He appeared, however, to have altered his opinion of his former sweetheart as she swore that he had given her the money to procure an abortion. Witnesses were called for both parties and the bench then made an order that Foster, whose wages were ten shillings a week, pay Annie Allen half a crown weekly for fourteen years and pay costs of two pounds fifteen shillings and the expenses of the order.

Men's offences against society did not necessarily include women. In December 1394 there was a male transvestite prostitute at large. The testimony of a John Rykener who called himself Eleanor, is recorded in Membrane 2 of Plea and Memoranda Roll A34, Corporation of London Records Office. He had been detained wearing women's clothing while having sex with another man in a London street one night in December 1394. He then moved to Oxford where he kept himself by doing embroidery and having sex with students. It is unclear whether these were consciously homosexual encounters or if Eleanor's partners had a colossal shock. He also claimed to have had sex with numerous women, including nuns, but not always for money. No records appear to have survived giving the outcome of the trial.

In the eighteenth century both Town and Gown were stunned by what was called '*l'Affaire* Wadham'. The Rev Robert Thistlethwayte, Warden of Wadham College was accused of making homosexual advances towards William French, one of his charges. French's tutor, John Swinton was similarly accused of homosexuality. This was not only scandalous but also a capital offence. All sorts of pamphlets and verses appeared on the subject. In 1737 Thistlethwayte left Wadham and took off for Boulogne. About this time the college took out fire insurance which provoked the rhyme:

> Well did the am'rous sone of Wadham
> Insure their house 'gainst future flame;
> They knew their crime, the crime of Sodom,
> And judg'd their punishment the same.

An anonymous limerick on the same subject runs:

> There once was a Warden of Wadham
> Who approved of the folkways of Sodom,
> For a man might, he said,
> Have a very poor head
> But be a fine Fellow, at bottom.

The unflattering nickname 'Wadhamite' continues to be used for members of the college.

Jackson's reported on 26 September 1874 that George Luker, a milkman employed by Mr Hicks of George Street, had been charged with committing an unnatural offence on the Botley Road one Sunday morning in a field belonging to Mr Pusey. The details of the case, says *Jackson's*, were unfit for publication, and after hearing them, the bench committed the prisoner for trial at the Assizes. It is unclear, therefore, if this was homosexual activity as no other man is mentioned as being involved; according to a few similar accounts, Luker could have been guilty of bestiality which was sometimes also reported as an unnatural act. Unfortunately, *Jackson's* does not report the outcome of the second trial.

From 4 November 1876: Thomas Digby, a servant at the prestigious Randolph Hotel, was charged with attempting to commit an unnatural act on 15-year-old Joseph Wood, in the urinal in Market Street about midnight one Saturday. The prisoner was freed the same night on ten pounds bail but as he failed to appear in court, a warrant was issued for his arrest.

From 22 June 1895: 56-year-old William James Toque, of no occupation, lodging in Marston Street, and William George Wilson, a painter aged 16, of Green Street, were charged, the first on remand, 'with committing an act of gross indecency contrary to the provisions of the Criminal Law Amendment Act on 10 June.'

When giving evidence, Toque's landlady, Mrs Elizabeth Roxbrough, stated that he had told her he was a retired doctor. About nine-thirty on the evening in question, she had heard someone come to the house, and then about half an hour later a bell rang. Believing it to be Toque, she went to his room where she was 'the witness of acts of indecency which she described.' He had brought the boy that she now identified as Wilson, home with him the previous week. On her entering the room, he had rushed out of the room. On hearing his wife scream, her husband had entered the room and asked Toque what he meant by bringing the boy there and committing such an act. Toque replied, 'I suppose you want money; what shall I give you?' Roxbrough said that he did not want money, and the next day informed the police. When apprehended at the Conservative Club, Toque denied the accusation but he was taken to the police station and formally charged. He contended that Wilson had a weak chest and he was examining him with a stethoscope. Both men were committed for trial at the Assize, only Wilson being allowed bail.

Jackson's continues the report the following week. Much was made of the fact that Toque was a gentleman, and according to testimonials 'strictly honourable'; the last, saying 'I believe him to be a man of excellent moral character' was, said the judge, 'rubbish and discreditable to the man who wrote it.' The judge then ranted on about Toque's possibility being 'the ruin, body and soul of that poor boy' who had 'tempted him to become a party to his filthy acts,' and the older man's 'evil hands'. He regretted that he could no longer transport him but he would pass as heavy a sentence as he was able 'not one day too heavy... and he hoped it might be a warning to others who were wickedly minded like himself not to indulge in these filthy practices...at the ruin of poor innocent boys.' The sentence was two years' imprisonment with hard labour. As for Wilson, his lenient punishment, for his own good, was imprisonment and hard labour for six months and 'at his age the sooner such actions were eradicated from his mind the better.'

What is considered offensive and of course what is legal or illegal, alters from century to century. A case in point is Parson's Pleasure, a section of the River Cherwell in the University Parks where male-only nude bathing used to take place until it was closed and was taken into the Parks in 1991. Adjoining Parson's Pleasure, the Rollers on this part of the river allowed boats to be raised from a lower section to a higher one. Any women in the boats had to get out and walk round the bathing place before getting back in the boat. Parson's Pleasure had a reputation, deserved or not, for its supposed homoerotic atmosphere. However, some might argue that the offences were really the fat and flabby flesh on display there, the misogyny and the inconvenience caused to other river users.

Chapter 9

Poverty and Charity

Until the measures leading to the creation of the welfare state in the twentieth century were put into place, anything done to help the destitute was on an ad hoc basis with largely personal funding.

Anthony Wood notes in December 1670 that beggars used to pray at people's doors for alms. This was an echo of pre-Reformation times when they prayed for their souls in exchange for food. But during times of religious contention, fanatics would not allow them to say prayers at their doors so that by the time of the Restoration in 1660, the practice died out. The last beggars to do so were Jack Saturday alias Williams and Meg Swiffin, a madwoman; they used to say their prayers at butchers' stalls, adds Wood.

Oxford had the usual range of facilities, including private contributions, for the poor, sick, elderly and insane but as elsewhere this was by no means always adequate. Some unfortunate people received no care and died as a consequence, others were reliant on donations. By 1854 charities for relieving the distressed included the Benevolent Society; the Soup and Coke Fund; the District Visiting Society; the Dorcas Society for supplying articles of dress to the poor; the Society for the Relief of Distressed Travellers and the Loan Society for advancing small loans to deserving poor. These were, of course, in addition to the workhouse and House of Industry for the eleven United Parishes of Oxford, and Headington union workhouse for the remainder of the city.

We are accustomed to accounts of the heartless attitudes to the provision of parish relief in general and the harshness of the workhouse in particular. We tend to overlook the never-ending demands that the individual gentleman had on his bank balance over and above the poor rate charges fixed by the parish itself, depending on the value of property owned or rented. Before the welfare state parishes might be overwhelmed by unforeseen tragedies and disasters which far exceeded their budgets and there were various ways that they managed to raise cash.

From its foundation in 1753 *Jackson's* contained regular entreaties ranging from requests for money for building and extending churches, founding schools, maintaining hospitals and asylums and numerous other public facilities, to immediate help for families and individuals.

In addition to the usual poor rate contributions, societies and institutions providing more formalized aid and support were opening up countrywide, frequently run by religious organizations and all dependent on voluntary contributions for their continuance. Among those in Oxford were the Female Penitentiary and the Refuge for Fallen Women, the Home of Compassion for Orphans and Foundlings' Home and the Anti-Mendicity Society. If they were sufficiently wealthy, Oxford residents would have been expected to become patrons, and if they were a landowner, to host fundraising events such as balls, concerts and garden parties.

In January 1763 a house-to-house collection was made by the leading residents of St Martin's parish 'for relieving the calamities of such of their industrious poor as endeavour [*sic*] by their own labour to avoid being burthensome to a parish, and whose distress in this rigorous season are worthy the attention of the charitable and humane.' *Jackson's* was sure that similar collections would be made all over the city and that there would be no need to force people to contribute. One item on which the money collected was spent was the roasting of a whole sheep on the thick ice near Hythe Bridge to which came a huge number of people. If the frost continued the following week an ox would be roasted on the River Isis below Folly Bridge.

Many examples of malnutrition and even starvation have come to light. In December 1679 the weather was exceptionally cold. A poor man died of starvation and exposure. 'He began to die in St Clement's parish' but when the parishioners discovered him, they put up two or three shillings to have him carried over Magdalen Bridge so that he died under the tower in the neighbouring parish, St Peter in the East so that they would not have to pay for the funeral. As late as 8 April 1755 a poor traveller was found dead at the corner of Holywell Street.

In December 1693 everything was so expensive and foodstuff scarce that thirty 'honest dwellers' in St Mary the Virgin parish were forced to beg for alms and weekly handouts as was the case in other parts of the city. Corn cost nine and sixpence a bushel and the poor ate turnips instead of bread.

From 4 December 1869: PC Keen discovered a man lying dead in Brooks's cowshed on the Botley Road, about two-thirty in the morning. The body was in an extraordinary state. It was stark naked, with a jacket laid across it and apart from the head was covered all over with hay. The face had turned almost black 'and presented a ghastly spectacle to the constable when he turned his bull's-eye upon it.' He had a colleague, Constable Jakeman, outside the cowshed and called out to him, 'Here's dead man!' At this, there was a movement in the hay and a man sprang out with a terrified cry of 'A dead man?'

'Yes,' replied PC Keen, and turned his lantern on the living man who made a dash for the door, as if running for his life. Jakeman recognized him as a local known as 'Juliana Johnson', who made a habit of sleeping rough in similar places and seemed to have been quite unconscious of the fact that he'd had a 'strange companion-sleeper lying a few feet from him and who slept the sleep of death.' The dead man's clothes were found among the hay: dirty shoes, the jacket, corduroy trousers, a little red scarf, black cotton braces, garters but no socks and no cash. The corpse was that of a tallish man, aged about 24, emaciated and weighing about eight and a half stone. The legs were in good condition but the stomach quite flat and the bones of the chest clearly defined. It was covered with vermin.

At an inquest held at the Hollybush Inn, a surgeon stated that the man had been dead some three or four days and had probably been suffering from consumption. Death had been caused by lack of food and possibly exposure. Had he been in the workhouse, or had something to eat, it was likely that he would still be alive. A post mortem was not considered necessary. The jury said that there was no doubt that the man had died 'of want', that is starvation. One member of the jury stated that 'there were plenty of people in Oxford now who were nearly in a starving state, and who would not go and say that they were in that condition' to the authorities.

From 1 April 1871: at an inquest, the coroner and jury heard of the death in the city gaol of 7-week-old Alfred Timms, the twin child of a widow who had been committed for neglecting her children. The puny body was in a pitiful state. The surgeon to the gaol, Mr George Taunton, said that he had seen the child when it was brought in a couple of days previously, apparently dying and in fact had only lived a few hours. The results of a post mortem showed that there was no disease or malformation of the body. It was 'perfectly destitute of fat and the stomach, &c all but empty.' It hardly weighed three and a half pounds when seven or eight pounds was normal.

The mother was healthy; the child had been given bread soaked in water as it refused to suckle. It was well clothed and kept clean. The other child was also likely to die. The relieving officer told the inquest that the mother had refused to go into the workhouse and he believed that she had had no handouts for more than a fortnight. The twins were illegitimate and he thought that they had been treated kindly but had been sickly from birth. The woman had two legitimate children who were at the Industrial School and a third at home.

He was told by the Guardians of the Poor to take the two children from the school to their home but as this was almost completely destitute, he approached the Reverend J. Rigaud and they were subsequently taken back to the workhouse where the third child joined them. The relieving officer added that he had seen the dead child fed with milk pap and afterwards with a little brandy. The jury returned a verdict in agreement with the medical evidence that they had heard.

An advertisement of 4 November 1865 reads:

> The Committee of the Home of Compassion for orphans and Foundlings, Howard Street, Iffley Road, earnestly beg Donations and Annual Subscriptions for the carrying on of this most necessary work for the prevention of Infanticide. Special offerings of warm clothing, either for bedding or wear as also toys, books, left-off wearing apparel, farinaceous and other foods, fitted for children, and coals towards the warming of the nurseries in winter, &c. thankfully received. Any one willing to take Donation Boxes, or Sixpenny Subscription Cards to fill up, can obtain them at the Home on application.
>
> Note: The Home is open for inspection every afternoon (Sundays excepted) from Three to Five.

However, in December 1866, inquests were held on a number of dead children at the Home of Compassion. Twin sisters Martha and Annie Smith were 'in a starved and otherwise neglected and ill-treated state';

Walter Scott had been suffering from bronchitis; Amelia Weatherby, who was admitted under protest, suffering from kidney disease and Ellen Mary Lucas, also with bronchitis. All the children had come from London.

The coroner said that he had himself ordered the inquest at the request of the overseers and churchwardens of the parish. It was certainly extraordinary that all these children should be dead at the home at the same time but this was a chance to find out the truth of the matter. In addition, it was strange that so many children should have died since the home was founded in May 1864. Since October 1865 the list provided by the Lady Superior showed that seventeen or eighteen had already died there. However, the mortality in comparable foundations including the Foundling Hospital in London, was considerably greater. It would be to the Home of Compassion's advantage to show that every care had been taken of its children.

The mayor remarked that as the majority of the children were the offspring of 'unfortunate women, they had the seeds of disease in their bodies when they were admitted to the home; their lives consequently were naturally of uncertain tenure.' Three of the four latest children were illegitimate. The medical officer confirmed that the twins in question had been weak and bordering on starvation when they were admitted and said Walter Scott had died of convulsions due to teething. Amelia's diet had been so bad that she was 'a fretful, poorly little thing, its legs were puffed up with dropsy and the mother did not expect it to survive the period of teething' while Ellen had been left by her mother 'to knock about on the floor' and had died of exhaustion.

After hearing a series of witnesses the jury decided that the children had died from natural causes and that the Home of Compassion was 'conducted in a most satisfactory manner, every care and attention being paid to the children entrusted to the Sisters.' To underline their approval, the jurymen donated their attendance fees to the home.

From 21 October 1871: Edward Clark, an undersized boy aged 10, who was living in Magdalen Road, was charged by PC Pancutt with begging in Marston Street with no visible means of support. The officer responsible for ensuring that children attended school stated that he had seen the boy begging on several occasions. His father was a mason's labourer who earned good wages. The representative of the School Board said that the Industrial School Act empowered the magistrates to look into the father's circumstances with a view to compel him to contribute to the maintenance of the boy and that there was a school in Bradford where he would be accepted free of charge. The boy was sent to the workhouse until the end of the week when his uncle promised that the father would attend the court.

At the end of December 1892 penny dinners started to be served in the town hall to the poor of the city. 'The committee of ladies having this laudable object in hand commenced supplying penny dinners from the kitchen of the Town Hall, and soup was provided for around 400 applicants.' On the following Tuesday, the number increased to well over 600, as it did on the Thursday, by which time word must have spread. However, 'the quantity of vegetables hitherto charitably given had been rather small and consequently it was found necessary to buy more largely than usual. Help both in money and in this respect will be thankfully received, and Miss Tawney of No. 63 St Giles-street is the treasurer of the fund.'

In February 1894 an inquest was held at the Horse and Chair public house in St Ebbe's before the city coroner on the body of Francis Hitchman, aged 70, of 5 Chaundy's Yard, who had worked as a French polisher. He had been found dead by his sister who lived with him. Instead of having the body taken to the mortuary as was usual, the coroner decided that the jury should see the location where the death had taken place. They found the corpse lying on a mattress in a first-floor room. Apart from a table in one corner, the room was empty of furniture and in a filthy state. The deceased's face was very thin, every rib plainly visible and the limbs and upper part of the body seemed literally nothing but skin and bone.

His sister, Ann Elizabeth Hitchman, was in a very weak condition. She told the jury that her brother had done very little work for a long time and that she had been obliged to keep them both by taking in sewing. Until recently he had been able to eat and drink fairly well but had been confined to his bed for the previous three weeks. He insisted on sleeping on the floor, refusing to have a bedstead. He had grown thinner by the day, sometimes too weak to get out of bed but refusing soup and other food, saying that he could not taste them. He refused to go to the Radcliffe Infirmary or have a doctor visit him. Unknown to him, his sister went to see the relieving officer in order to have Francis taken to the workhouse but he was not at home.

One of the jurymen stated that the Hitchmans' house was not fit for habitation. One of the neighbours remarked that cleanliness depended on the residents and that her own was very different. A verdict of 'Death from natural decay, accelerated by the want of the necessaries of life,' was returned.

A sudden and unexpected change of circumstance might mean destitution. The consequences of the ultimate, if involuntary, form of desertion can be found in the following series of advertisements for the bereaved who found it difficult, if not impossible, to cope with life without their spouses. The organizers of such appeals often published the names of contributors with the amounts that they had given, for they were astute enough to realize that while some wished to remain anonymous, the remainder would serve as both an endorsement of the worthiness of the venture and as a means of extracting the maximum amount of those who wished to keep up with, or even exceed, the donation made by the Joneses.

Squeezed in below a notice of cancellation of Oxford races is this pathetic appeal dated 14 July 1821:

SUBSCRIPTIONS for the distressed WIDOW and ELEVEN CHILDREN of JOHN PUGH
Coach-maker, deceased

Amount already received:	£24. 2.6d
Dr Williams:	£ 1. 1. 0d
Subscriptions by Mr Gurdon:	£ 2. 0. 0d
Miss Fisher:	£ 0. 7. 6d
Miss B:	£ 0. 7. 6d

This appeal appeared on 22 February1823:

TO THE CHARITABLE AND HUMANE

A Case of extreme Distress
On the 19th instant, HENRY GOODWYN, Shoemaker, of the Corn Market, Oxford, in a fit of insanity, occasioned by the embarrassed state of his affairs, put a period to his existence by dividing the carotid artery by which dreadful circumstance his WIDOW and EIGHT CHILDREN,

Five of whom are under Eleven years of age, the eldest only Fourteen, are left totally destitute of the means of support, without money, without food, and without any friends whose situation in life can enable them to assist her.

Under these circumstances, some benevolent individuals have suggested that an appeal to the charitable feelings of the public in behalf of the distressed widow and family would not be made in vain.

Owing to the bad state of Mr Goodwyn's affairs, he had long been unable to execute the orders of his customers, and but faint hopes are entertained that any permanent advantage can be derived from a continuation of the Business. This, however, will rest with the benevolent persons who may be induced to come forward in alleviation of such unparalleled distress – distress which leaves no alternative but that of public charity, or a consignment of herself and hapless children to the shelter of the Poor House! It is earnestly hoped that this last alternative may be averted; and that the Widow, who has always borne the character of an honest and industrious wife, and a good mother, may be enabled, by the benevolence of the public, in conjunction with her own industry, to rear her family, and render them useful and respectable members of society in the situations in which they may be placed.

The Rev Mr Barter of New college and the Rev Mr Dornford of Oriel college, have kindly undertaken to act as Trustees and they propose: -

1st. To provide present necessaries
2nd. To apply a Sum for re-commencing Business
3rd. To reserve small allotments for apprenticing the Daughters

There follows a two-column list of people who had contributed to the Oxford banks. The amounts range from five guineas to a pound and the subscribers include the Bishop of Oxford, several heads of house and one or two anonymous individuals.

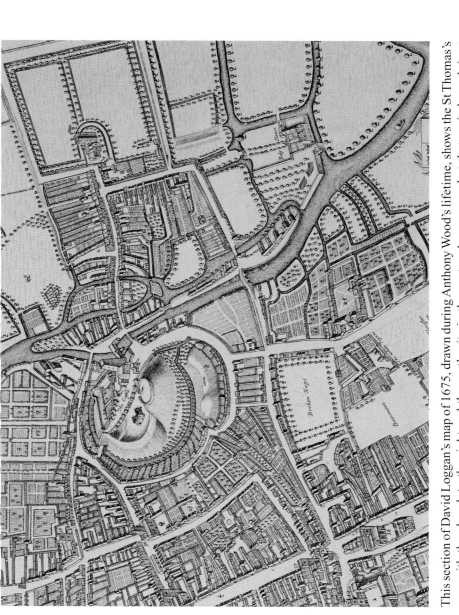

This section of David Loggan's map of 1675, drawn during Anthony Wood's lifetime, shows the St Thomas's area with the church to the right and the castle site in the centre. As was usual at that period, north is at the bottom.

A very detailed 1876 Ordnance Survey map of the western part of Oxford that features largely in the book, much of which has long been redeveloped. The station, public houses and breweries are prominent as is the prison and the rows of squalid little terraced houses.

The cobbled Norman crypt of Oxford Castle is said to attract gatherings of the spirits that haunt the building and previously unseen dark figures are visible when photographs including a particular corner are examined.

Ruins of Osney Abbey. This Augustinian foundation, one of the greatest in the country, dominated the western outskirts of the town and was the single most serious loss to Oxford of the many religious foundations that disappeared at the Dissolution of the Monasteries.

OXFORD GASLIGHT AND COKE COMPANY

Aerial view of St Ebbe's, one of Oxford's poorer parishes dominated by the production of the city's gas supply until the last of the gas-holders was demolished in 1968.

Excessive drinking was by no means confined to the lower classes. On 7 February 1691, John Forster, Fellow of prestigious All Souls College, died late at night after 'immoderate drinking' at the ancient Mitre Hotel and was buried in the college's outer chapel.

The Mercury Fountain in Christ Church's Tom Quad was a rallying point for members of the college and also the dumping ground for the door knockers and trophies stolen by undergraduate pests in 1835.

An eighteenth-century view of the area around Oxford Castle, from *The New British Traveller, or a Complete Modern Universal Display of Great Britain and Ireland* 1784. It shows the mound that formed part of the original Norman construction.

Above: These men employed in road repairs in Broad Street are using stones obtained by the hard labour to which prisoners in the castle were committed.

Left: The eleventh-century St George's Tower still looms over St Thomas's. It is possible to climb to the top as part of a castle tour.

St Mary Hall, now part of Oriel College, where Francis Suckling stole a fellow undergraduate's cash in order to go Christmas shopping in December 1885 and ended up in prison.

The second St Martin's, or Carfax, church that replaced the medieval one in 1822, shortly before its demolition in 1896 as an obstacle to traffic, leaving only the medieval tower that still survives. The crossroads has been a meeting place for hundreds of years.

When it was opened in 1897, the present town hall was the scene of a riot that spread to the surrounding streets.

The riot and massacre on 10 February 1355, St Scholastica's Day, as represented in the Oxford Pageant in 1908. This postcard shows the date 1354 as according to the old calendar the year started on Lady Day, 25 March.

The Divinity School, now part of the Bodleian Library complex, was the scene of the trial of Miss Mary Blandy prior to her execution in the castle for poisoning her father.

THE OLDEST HOUSE IN OXFORD (13th century)
The Octagon House, Broad Street.
(Formerly a bastion in the old City Wall and then known as "Our Ladye's Chappel at Smithgate").

The Smith Gate, one of the medieval entrances to the town, was the scene of the murder of William de Burford by James de Hybernia which appears in the records of the 1285 eyre.

Above left: Known in the Middle Ages as Grope**** Lane, then Magpie Lane from an alehouse once situated there, then Grape Lane from the seventeenth century and Grove Street in Victorian times, this little street is once again called Magpie Lane.

Above right: Narrow, high-walled New College Lane, leading to the college and built on what had been waste ground frequented by thieves and prostitutes, is still found oppressive by some people today.

The Clarendon Building housed the press of the same name until it moved to Walton Street in 1832. After this it was the base for the university police and prostitutes were locked in its basement. It is now part of the Bodleian Library.

Paradise Square where, in December 1857, schoolteacher John Sixsmith was robbed by a prostitute while, he was relieving himself against a wall.

Adjoining Parson's Pleasure, the Rollers on this part of River Cherwell let boats be raised from a lower section to a higher one. All females had to get out of the boats and walk round the bathing place before getting back in.

An example of the city's
cramped dwellings in courtyards
and alleyways – Hell's Passage
was the home of Jane Burden
who married Pre-Raphaelite,
William Morris at St Michael at
the North Gate on 26 April 1859.
Nowadays it is better known as
the entrance to the Turf Tavern.

Below: Originally a leper
hospital, St Bartholomew's
Hospital, often called Bartlemas,
is shown here in 1832, when it
was the House of Convalescence
during the cholera outbreak
that year.

BALLIOL COLLEGE, OXFORD.

Cab rank in Broad Street outside Balliol College. Anyone travelling in such a flimsy vehicle would not stand much of a chance if involved in a collision.

St. Giles Fair, Oxford.

St Giles's Fair: this seemingly innocent event involved anti-social behaviour, ruined reputations and fatal falls.

THE DEER PARK, MAGDALEN COLLEGE, OXFORD.

Descendants of the deer that clustered around the body of the Rev G. Grantham when he broke his neck falling from his window in May 1840 can still be seen in Magdalen Deer Park today.

The Cloisters, Magdalen College, Oxford

Magdalen cloisters where the body of James Barne was brought after he was shot by an unknown person while in a boat on the Cherwell in May 1868.

The spot between hall and chapel in Oriel Front Quad is where John Key landed after his fatal fall from the leads in1849.

It is easy to see why the Isis and the Cherwell were so dangerous when packed with crafts of all sorts and hundreds of onlookers; the well-dressed lady standing up in the punt would have been particularly at risk if there had been an accident.

ST ALBAN HALL
N. Whittock Lith.d Oxford.

St Alban Hall, now part of Merton College,
where Henry Abbott committed suicide
by shooting himself in his rooms in
December 1826.

St Frideswide's shrine was destroyed when
St Frideswide's Priory was suppressed in 1538
and the pieces thrown down a well. These were
rediscovered and the shrine rebuilt in 1891 with
a second reconstruction in 2002.

The Botanic Garden occupies part of the site of the medieval Jewish burial ground, at that time outside the town walls.

St Mary Magdalen church, site of the burial of suicides and a thwarted attempt at grave-robbing, from *Memorials of Oxford*, John Le Keux (1783-1846) published by John Henry Parker, Oxford 1837. Drawing is by F. Mackenzie.

'Skeleton Corner', as the Anatomy School at Christ Church was nicknamed, shown in 1821 from *The University and City of Oxford in a Series of Seventy Two Views Drawn and Engraved by J & H.S. Storer etc.*

From 7 January 1832:

Affecting Case of Distress
THE Widow and Nine Young Children of the late
Mr. WENTWORTH, Surgeon-Apothecary, of Oxford,
are left by his decease in a state of utter destitution. After
several years considerable practice in his profession, he
had to struggle for a long period under the pressure of
declining health, and the claims of an increasing family;
but having sunk at length under the combined effects of
sickness and adversity, his bereaved Widow and helpless
Orphans are left with no resource but an appeal to the
generous sympathies of a humane and benevolent public,
through whose prompt and liberal assistance it is proposed
to raise a Fund, by Subscription, sufficient to enable the
afflicted Widow to embark in some line of business, by
which she may be enabled to supply the wants of her
numerous family.

Subscriptions will be received at all the Oxford
Banks; at Messrs Jones and Lloyd's, Bankers, London;
by Mr Hitchings, Surgeon, and Mr Webb, Surgeon and
Apothecary, Oxford, who have kindly consented to act as
trustees.

A long list of subscriptions, with names and amounts follows.
In the same edition, subscriptions were requested for providing the
'Industrious Poor with employment and also to afford assistance to such
of the aged and infirm as are really necessitous.'
From 15 August 1835:

TO THE CHARITABLE

ROBERT GUEST, late of the New Inn, St Aldates, Oxford,
being left a widower with a family of five children, under
14 years of age and now entirely out of employ, and in great
distress, humbly solicits the assistance of the charitable and
humane, to enable him to get into a small way of business,
to support his family. Mr W Cooke and Mr T Mallam have

kindly undertaken to receive and expend the same for their benefit. The smallest sum will be thankfully received at the Bank of Messrs. Morrell.

Mr T Mallam £1   Mr W Cooke 10s

On 23 March 1839 this appeal to the hearts of the public appeared:

This appeal is made on behalf of FOUR ORPHAN CHILDREN, three sons and a daughter of the late R.H. Guest, for many years landlord of the New Inn in Oxford. Who expired after a painful illness on 26th February last, under most distressing and heartrending circumstances, which if generally known would excite the charity of all charitable and humane persons – having had the whole of his furniture &c distrained on the 19th December last for a small sum due for rent, since which day he with three of his children (until within a week of his death) lay on the floor with scarcely any thing to cover them and without the common necessities of life. The object of this appeal to the public is to raise a sum sufficient to place the children at school for a limited period during which time it is hoped the necessity of these unfortunate orphans becoming inmates of the workhouse. Mr T. Mallam, High-street, Mr W. Thorpe, Holywell-street and Mr T. Dry, Pembroke-street, have kindly consented to receive subscriptions and apply them for the benefit of the children.

From 22 May 1841: one morning James Best Finmere, a journeyman cabinet-maker aged 52, was delivering some work that he had completed to the house of Mr Herbert, another cabinet-maker. As they were talking, James Finmere suddenly dropped to the ground, dead. He had been subject to shortness of breath for many years and the verdict at the inquest was 'Died suddenly by the visitation of God.' Because of this dreadful visitation, a widow and eight children were left without a kind and loving parent by whose sudden death the family was left wholly destitute with no means of support. An appeal was set up 'to the charitable and humane on behalf of the widow and children'. Mr W. Herbert at

31 Cornmarket Street and Mr W. Thurland at 16 Ship Street offered to receive contributions and put them to the best possible use for the needs of the bereaved family.

From 5 October 1889:

> To the Editor
> SIR, - Permit me to appeal for aid for the widow of a steady young man, John White, gardener, aged 25 years, who was accidentally drowned near the Weirs on Tuesday last. She is left almost destitute, with two little children. We wish to raise a fund to help her to begin to support herself and them.
> Donations of any amount will be thankfully received by Mr George Brunner, 39, New Inn Hall-street, or by
>
> Yours faithfully,
> HALSALL SEGAR
> Vicar of South Hincksey
> New Hincksey Vicarage, Sept. 28

For centuries, as now, homelessness was an unpalatable fact of Oxford life. Wood notes in 1661:

> 'Old mother Slye, an Oxford huckster, dying in a frosty and snowy season, Georg Payne, the witty and waggish cook of St Alban's hall made this epitaph on her:
> Death came by
> And struck mother Sly
> A deep and deadly blow:
> He took her o' the eare
> With a greate orange peare
> And kil'd her in the midst of the snow.'

This advertisement appeared in *Jackson's* on 2 April 1887:

THE FIRE IN PARADISE SQUARE
To the EDITOR of the OXFORD JOURNAL

DEAR SIR, - You will oblige me by inserting the following appeal on behalf of Mrs Joy, who has just suffered a very serious loss through a fire which broke out in her house this morning. She is a laundress, and is 74 years of age.

I am, dear Sir, yours faithfully.
JOHN ARKELL
St Ebbe's Rectory, Oxford, March 31, 1887

We, the Rector and Churchwardens of the Parish of St Ebbe, having heard with regret of the loss sustained by Mrs Joy, a laundress of 7, Paradise-square, through a fire which has completely destroyed the whole of her laundry, and rendered her for the time homeless and almost destitute, will gladly receive and apply for her benefit, any contributions which kind friends may entrust to them for her. We estimate the loss at 20l.

JOHN ARKELL Rector
HENRY GUISE
GEORGE HOPCROFT Churchwardens

From 1 December 1877: patrons were sought for a foundation that was not as well known or supported as others because its work was 'carried on in a very quiet and unostentatious manner.' The Oxford Refuge for Fallen Women had been opened some three years previously by two Oxford clergymen as a 'Preparatory Home in connection with the long-established Penitentiary in Holywell'. It was believed that if such a place of safety was not made available 'their evil associates [were] certain to regain a hold on them.'

However, a new lifestyle could only be achieved with a considerable amount of time and patience. Rehabilitation and training for a respectable position took two years minimum as it had been shown that this was the length of time necessary to adjust from 'an existence of utter lawlessness and excitement' to 'the religious calm and strict discipline of a regularly organised Home.' Even so, it was suspected that the change might turn out to be 'too sudden for their wayward and impulsive temperaments'. The refuge doors remained open day and night, 'as it is generally under cover of darkness that these poor wanderers resort to those who they have reason to hope will assist them.' Inmates of the refuge were often given laundry work and the payment they received for this helped towards the cost of running the institution.

Poverty appears to often have been viewed as an offence, if not a crime. For example in *Jackson's* of 27 September 1879, a tramp called Mary Ann Dell pleaded guilty to sleeping out in a privy in Hart's Yard, St Ebbe's one Sunday morning with no visible means of subsistence. A police constable stated that a considerable number of complaints had been received about tramps sleeping in this building. She received seven days' hard labour.

From 26 September 1885: at the city police court Sophia Stone, a married woman, was charged with sleeping in a doorway in Worcester Terrace at one-forty in the morning and with having no visible means of subsistence. PC Mortimore stated that Stone had already been convicted four times of similar offences, the last earning her a month in gaol. The mayor said that he had advised Stone to go into the workhouse as her husband was barely able to keep himself; as she refused to go there she must go to gaol for a month, with hard labour.

At the same court homeless Robert Adams was charged with being found wandering abroad in Castle Street at one-thirty that same morning and also having no visible means of subsistence. PC Phillips said that all that Adams had on him was tobacco, pipe and matches. The prisoner said that neither his mother nor his wife would allow him to sleep at either of their homes. When the clerk asked his age, he first said that he would be 15 next week and then admitted that he was 29. He had been convicted four times since the last December, and was then sentenced to one month's hard labour.

From 6 February 1886: one Sunday evening a homeless married woman named Sarah Stone, an old offender, was charged with being found sleeping in a doorway in St Giles and having no visible means of subsistence. She pleaded guilty, being forced to be where she was found. Her daughter, a Mrs Belcher, told the bench that she would look after her mother as long as she would stay with her, and on that condition she was discharged.

From 15 February 1890: Mary Ann Clark, a homeless charwoman, was charged with having been found sleeping on premises in Worcester Street with no visible means of subsistence at three-thirty-five that morning. She pleaded guilty and PC Goddard stated that he had found her asleep. There had already been complaints of people sleeping rough in the area. Clark was given seven days' hard labour.

From 30 July 1892: Henry Sims, a tramp of no fixed abode, was charged with begging from house to house in Abbey Road one Saturday morning. Sims replied that he had been looking for work. PC Barrett stated that he had seen the prisoner coming out of a passage and when asked what he was doing there had been told that he was begging for water. Barrett took him back to the house and learnt that Sims had been begging for food. The occupier of one of the houses told the constable that Sims was often there and had become a real nuisance. Sims said that he was quite sure that he had never been there before, but was sentenced to four days' imprisonment with hard labour.

From 10 February 1894: Charles Kimber, described as a tramp, was charged with being drunk and begging from house to house in Queen Street one Monday evening. PS Prior stated that Kimber had been thrown out of the Queen's Restaurant and then went into the smoking room at the Three Cups. When he left, the police officer followed him into The Sun and arrested him while he was in the act of begging. Kimber said that he was an actor who had played in Mr Cooper's pantomime at the old theatre some years previously. Now, however, he was getting on in years and there was no longer much demand for his services. He had become very weak for lack of food and was 'more fit for a hospital than anything else'. The mayor said that the magistrates were inclined to believe that he had seen better days and that he would be sentenced to one day's imprisonment in the hope that he would return to his friends in London. The prisoner replied, 'Thank you, sir.'

Poverty in Oxford, and the reaction to it, is well documented but one aspect remains hidden. This is the genteel poverty, the middle-class poor who did not qualify for handouts, but had to contribute to the upkeep of paupers whether deserving or undeserving. These luckless Oxonians struggled desperately to keep their heads above water and keep their way of life and social status.

Chapter 10

Disease

In the *Wadham College Gazette*, January 2013, Dr Allan Chapman summed up the situation in Oxford over the centuries:

> 'We must remember that until the improvement of public health and the development of more reliable medicine in the nineteenth century, all schools, colleges, monasteries, and legal and ecclesiastical chapters routinely suffered death rates that would be unimaginable today.
>
> 'Just think, if during your undergraduate career in Oxford, an epidemic of typhus fever, smallpox, enteric fever, sweating sickness, or bubonic plague had descended and suddenly killed off some of your friends! Or just imagine losing a colleague to "phthisis" (pulmonary tuberculosis), an acute gastric condition caused by a dirty kitchen or rotten food, a "wasting away", a "great headache" (perhaps meningitis), or septicaemia from a cut! Yet all these things were part of "normal" life 400 years ago.'

Researchers into the history of disease in Oxford are fortunate that many sources, civic, ecclesiastical and academic, survive. The first known reference to an infectious disease in Oxford is a twelfth-century record of leprosy in the leper hospital of St Bartholomew; this is ironic in view of the fact that, during the cholera outbreak of 1832, this same building was to become the city's convalescent house.

In early modern times, people took a lively interest in both illness and weather conditions and by the mid-seventeenth century doctors and scientists were trying to establish some connection between them. Writers began to question why diseases varied according to locality and time of year, why certain environments were healthier than others and whether knowledge of such matters could improve health.

Particularly informative are seventeenth-century sources which include those generated by the royalist garrison stationed in the city and the Royal Court which resided in Oxford from 1642-46. By far the most fascinating, however, are the writings of Anthony Wood, who kept a record of his life and times from 1632 to 1695.

Wood cites an early example of the unsanitary conditions prevalent in the town, but in this case with some most unexpected offenders. He describes the court in Oxford in 1666, 'to give further character of the court, though they were neat and gay in their apparel, yet they were very nasty and beastly, leaving at their departure their excrements in every corner, in chimneys, studies, coal-houses, cellars. Rude, rough, whoremongers; vain, empty and careless.'

Parish registers indicate a slight drop in population, more pronounced in some parishes than in others, in the early decades of the nineteenth century, although this could well be a case of under-recording as everyone was buried, whereas by no means all parishioners were baptized.

It is unlikely that we shall ever be able to gain more than an impression of the causes of illness and death. For example, phthisis was the biggest single killer in nineteenth-century Oxford, surpassing even cholera itself during the epidemic of 1849.

Records from the Middle Ages contain many references to mysterious diseases which dispatched the residents of Oxford suddenly and inexplicably. It is impossible to ascertain what these are likely to have been, apart from those outbreaks which were almost certainly plague or one of the assorted fevers rife until modern times. The best the medical historian can attempt is an educated guess based on examination of what can be deduced from clues available, namely the season of the year during which the outbreak took place, or the age and sex of victims.

Plague is the most outstanding of all diseases known to Europe. It has entered our folk history and its dramatic impact is perpetuated in accounts of the Black Death and the Great Plague of London in 1665. Bubonic plague is almost certainly the only disease of which everyone could name the symptoms. The name 'plague' is colloquially and historically applied to any epidemic disease with a high mortality rate, but today it usually refers to the bubonic plague.

DISEASE

The best documented Oxford epidemic, the so-called Black Death, (the name was first used in England in the early nineteenth century but was not current at the time, being referred to simply as 'the Death'), attacked a town already in decline. As elsewhere, the immediate impact was devastating, although we have no means of telling how many scholars were killed. Indeed the total numbers of the university overall throughout the Middle Ages is likely to remain an enigma; contemporary figures, like the majority of medieval accounts, are certainly exaggerated. Oxford may have lost approximately one third of its population and it was necessary for in-migration from the surrounding countryside to remain high for some considerable time afterwards to compensate for the depleted workforce.

The disease reached Oxford in November 1348 and lasted until the following June. Rent rolls show many vacant academic halls and numerous empty tofts even in the main streets immediately after the epidemic receded. Distinguished victims included two mayors, Richard Sellwood and Richard Cary, the Abbess of Godstow, the Prioress of Littlemore, two chancellors of the university and two provosts of Oriel College. Seven of Oxford's fourteen parishes had a change of incumbent between April and December 1349, at least five of these vacancies being due to death.

That many Oxford residents contracted plague is shown by a minimum of fifty-seven wills made during the epidemic and entered in the town's register [*Liber albus civitatis oxoniensis. Abstract of the Wills, Deeds and Enrolments contained in the White Book of the City of Oxford,* W. P. Ellis, pp. 35-57], the previous average number being three or four wills annually. Mortality was particularly high in January 1349, with ten wills, peaking to sixteen in April and declining to only two in June, which indicated that the plague was pneumonic rather than bubonic which is at its worst in hot, dry months. Ten years later in 1359 came one of the worst outbreaks of all, when sixteen fatal cases occurred in a single day and colleges were forced to close.

The year 1361 also proved lethal with eleven enrolled wills [*Ibid*, 56] as were 1370-1, 1406-7, most years between 1448 and 1463, 1478, p. 1485-9, 1493 and 1499, as shown by records compiled by Merton College, by the congregation of the university and by the mortuary payments from the parishes of All Saints and St Michael at the North Gate where there were 117 deaths.

In 1478 the proctors were paid a bonus on account of the dangers involved in carrying out their duties. [Medieval Archives of the University of Oxford, edited H.E. Salter, iii, *Oxford Historical Society*, LXXIII, 1919, p. 281]. In 1492, following a dearth year after the exceptionally hard winter of 1490, there were forty-six deaths, although, in Merton records this was not recorded as a plague year. [*Registrum Annalium Coll Merton*, p. 126].

By 1493 the university seems to have lost patience with Oxford's unhealthy location for the suggestion was advanced that its masters and scholars leave permanently and settle somewhere healthier. The majority of the colleges had already established plague-houses locally and so accustomed had the university become to this procedure it decreed that the time spent elsewhere during plague-time might be counted as equivalent to residing in Oxford for the necessary number of terms 'kept' to become eligible for a degree.

Although the worst plague epidemic was over by then, the late-fourteenth century saw the outset of a new, short-lived and still unexplained epidemic disease, known as the 'English sweats', or just the 'sweats'. In Oxford in 1518 houses with victims living in them were ordered to be distinguished by a display of straw outside. It continued into the sixteenth century, only to subside before it disappeared for ever.

Sixteen years of the sixteenth century are actually recorded as those during which epidemics occurred. Most of them are of bubonic plague, among the most deadly being that of 1571 with deaths being four times the usual figure. The most spectacular and long-remembered Oxford epidemic was the phenomenon of the Black Assize of 1577, when more than 300 people, including the Chief Baron of the Exchequer, Sir Robert Bell and the high sheriff were killed by a mysteriously virulent outbreak of something which may or may not have been bubonic plague. Under the circumstances it is likely to have been typhus, justifying its other name of gaol fever [*Oxford City Records*, p. 429].

In a bid to clean up the city, the cottages next to the schools were demolished in 1582 as plague nests, and the Mayor of Oxford wrote to his London counterpart requesting that Londoners coming to Oxford to attend St Frideswide's Fair carry certificates of good health to lessen the chance of infection arriving with them. [A. Wood, The University of Oxford, iii, *Oxford Historical Society*, XVI, 1889, pp. 211-12] In 1593 further attempts included the removal of garbage and pigs from Oxford's streets, restrictions on strangers staying in lodgings and a clampdown on plays and games. That year the crowd gathered in Oxford for the Universities Act, or degree ceremony, was blamed for an outbreak of plague. [*Ibid,* ii, 254]

Remarkably, the seventeenth-century university archivist, Brian Twyne, wrote of Oxford's 'reputation for healthiness' [Bodl Ms Twyne xxiv, p. 295], while surrounded with the living evidence of so much disease, in particular plague and smallpox. Plague was a hazard again in 1603, the city churches were closed for a time in 1625-6, for which parliament's arrival in Oxford was blamed [Wood, *Op cit,* ii (1) pp. 279-80, 355] and again during the civil wars of the 1640s when taxes for the relief of victims were collected on a regular basis and isolation cabins constructed for their use on Port Meadow, where the cholera hospital was to be built in 1832. This practice dates back to at least 1624-5 when 'chamberlains' were given fifty pounds to construct similar cabins.

By early 1643 the Royalists had settled in Oxford, which, along with the rest of the Thames Valley was of great strategic importance to both them and the opposing parliamentary army. There was a great deal of communication between Oxford, London and Reading, as Oxford resumed the role which it had played in its infancy as a frontier town and crossroads.

A 'bill of all that deceased during the week 18th to 25th October 1644', survives in Wood [Bodleian Ms Wood 514 (15a)] 'this and the year following being those of plague'. Parliament met again at Oxford in 1665, when the Great Plague was raging in London, but Oxford suffered less severely than the capital.

Typhoid fever is an acute infectious disease caused by the typhoid *bacillus* which is transmitted by milk, water, or solid food contaminated by faeces of typhoid victims or of carriers, healthy persons who harbour typhoid bacilli without presenting symptoms.

From 8 February 1852: at a meeting regarding the drainage of the Thames, it was said 'that in considerable areas ague has been very prevalent in the memory of man, and is now unknown; low fever (mild typhoid) having taken its place.'

From 15 May 1858: the workhouse was attacked by an outbreak of typhoid of a particularly virulent type as no less than eight inmates had died from it. The Poor Law inspector said that there was no doubt that this was due to overcrowding.

From 4 December 1875: at a meeting Mr Wootten, surgeon, claimed that typhoid was being spread all over the city, especially via the sewers. 'This was the case with Prince Leopold. He lived in Oxford perfectly safe until his house was connected with the drains of the town, and then he caught the fever, and that was a fact.'

From 16 April 1881: 'We are glad to learn that the Hon. A. Parker, who has recently been suffering from a severe attack of typhoid fever at Oxford, has so far progressed towards convalescence, that his removal to Shirburn Castle was safely accomplished on Saturday, and inquiries on Monday showed that he had in no way suffered from the fatigue of the journey. Lady Elizabeth Parker, who caught the fever from her brother, still lies at Oxford, but by the latest accounts is progressing favourably.'

Before the development of bacteriology, typhoid was frequently confused with typhus. This name is given to any one of a group of infectious diseases caused by bacteria transmitted by lice, fleas, mites and ticks. Symptoms include fever, headache and rash. The most serious form is epidemic typhus, which also affects the brain, heart, lungs and kidneys and is associated with unsanitary, overcrowded conditions.

Sir Samuel Luke writes in July 1643 'that there dyes about 40 a weeke of the plague [the editor's footnote reads *"morbus campestris"*] in Oxford, besides many of other diseases.' In August, he writes 'That the Queen is in Oxford and very sick and that they dye 20 a day of the sickness.' [The Journal of Sir Samuel Luke, 1643-4, vol i, *Oxfordshire Record Society,* XXIX, 1947, p. 114] In December of the same year: 'That there are many dye days in Oxford of the new disease (as they call it),' [*Ibid* 130, 140] that autumn. In these cases, if the disease had been plague, occurring in the autumn it would have been pneumonic rather than bubonic, but 'war typhus' has plague-like symptoms of buboes and spots and these had been noted among the victims during the hot summer of that year.

This new disease, which was indeed that known as camp, or gaol, fever, was probably typhus, which is known to affect adults more than children and this is supported by the burial registers. It features largely in the 1640s, although E. Greaves's *Morbus Epidemus*, of 1643, [Bodleian Library, Antiq e 1643 p. 66] claims that its virulence was considerably lower than that of plague and that rotten food rather than famine accounted for many deaths. The *Victoria County History of Oxfordshire* [*VCH Oxon,* vol iv, p. 118] states that it was the poor of Oxford rather than the community as a whole who felt the impact of disease, but an examination of the experiences of both the university in general and of individual colleges indicates otherwise. A late-nineteenth-century contributor to the *Oxford Magazine* [vol 10, No 9, of 10 February 1892, pp. 162-3] was 'prompted by a recent influenza epidemic which forced postponement of Term', to submit an article entitled, 'Seventeenth-Century Epidemics in Oxford', which he has extracted from Wood's entries, 1660-1695.

Throughout his life Wood exhibited a lively interest in maladies of all kinds, in particular the plagues and fevers which the seventeenth century was so prone to and lists his own afflictions in great detail, even venturing to suggest reasons for their origins. He suffered from a depressingly protracted series of agues which sound suspiciously like bouts of malaria [*The Life and Times of Anthony Wood*, edited A. Clark, 1961, p. 225], although he discards this idea in favour of blaming the weather. Disappointingly, he makes no mention of having been bitten by a mosquito prior to any of his ague attacks and refrains from commenting on the implications of a plague of flying ants in hot weather.

Identifying fevers is by no means straightforward. Ague is one of the types of fever mentioned most frequently by early modern writers, including Shakespeare. Thomas Willis, the Oxford-trained physician, refers to fevers in mid-century as that 'army of pestiferous diseases'.

Although it was the cause of great suffering during the Middle Ages, it was not until the eighteenth century that malaria, from *mal aria*, the Italian for bad air, gradually replaced the name ague. Malaria is caused by the female *anopheles atroparvus* mosquito which transmits a parasite to man. In the seventeenth and eighteenth centuries, waves of malaria swept across Europe, emanating from epidemic centres, low-lying badly-drained areas where mosquitoes bred in the stagnant water which they needed to lay their eggs. Oxford was, and to a certain extent still is, notorious for the amount of surface water in the area which causes respiratory conditions.

In the winter of 1660-61 there was sickness in New College which became so bad that on 3 December its Fellows were forced to leave and go home. This outbreak is believed to have been the spotted or purple fever, which might have been scarlet fever, while in the autumn of 1661 a new disease, a strange fever, or feverish distemper raged in the town.

A strange fever swept the whole country in 1670, and an unusual one, termed a new disease in October 1672, raged with great resultant morbidity. That month and the next an odd pestilential fever appeared bringing several deaths. It was malignant and, according to Wood, little better than plague. Young men and children were most susceptible and many died; there were six deaths at Wadham alone, as appear in the Holywell burial records, with a further three at Christ Church and one at Oriel.

Spring 1684 brought agues of several descriptions and in high summer the pestilential fever claimed many victims. Odd fevers came in 1685-6, from December until April and smallpox continued among the young from November to March, when several Fellows of Corpus Christi College fled from it. The Act, as the degree ceremony was then known, of July 1688 was cancelled due to an epidemic fever which had attacked most colleges from June onwards, while 1691 brought a new malignant fever which killed many during August and was followed by an 'exceedingly fatal' bout of smallpox. Measles seems to have become something of a childhood disease by 1693 when it was very frequent in Oxford, and yet another unusual fever appeared in November, which lasted until February 1694 and 'was not understood by physicians a good while.' The reason for a very malignant fever to which Wadham College fell victim in 1734 seemed easy to find for it was agreed that the contagious infection arose from the putrefaction of a large quantity of cabbages thrown out into a heap from the several gardens near Wadham.

The autumn of 1662 saw smallpox at New College and in the spring of 1665 there were eleven cases resulting in five deaths at Lincoln College. This disease returned in 1667 and was very common in the town in the spring of 1668 and returned from June to Christmas 1674, while the next May to August saw a particularly deadly outbreak, seizing mostly upon citizens' children. The university was very empty in the Long Vacation and many failed to return in October, preferring to stay with friends, or outside the city. Similarly, in October and November 1675 smallpox was commonplace among children; colds and fevers were also rife, resulting in a number of deaths.

Smallpox returned in August and September 1683, so that the university was once more empty, some leaving the town that would not have gone under normal circumstances. Several parishes experienced deaths and Londoners, who were among the town's most frequent visitors, were afraid to come to Oxford. The epidemic continued into mid-November, when some parishes ordered tolling bells to cease as they were felt to be detrimental to trade.

The Act (or degree ceremony) was again cancelled in 1694 and that autumn brought fatal smallpox. The next spring was a most unnatural season, with more deaths, despite the continuing cold and August and September 1695 saw smallpox rife among scholars.

Smallpox continued to be a habitual feature of Oxford life during the eighteenth century and the years 1710, 1719 and 1728 were notable. (Thomas Hearne, *Collections,* x, pp. 162-3) Although today we are accustomed to thinking that Edward Jenner's development of vaccination spelled the end for smallpox, both this practice and the older one of inoculation met with fierce opposition from both the city and the university. *Jackson's* carries a range of announcements and advertisements concerning practitioners of inoculation working in the county, most of them well away from Oxford, although in 1768, one practitioner held a surgery in the King's Arms in Holywell every Saturday from noon until three in the afternoon.

In 1772, the university's Newdigate Prize for English Verse was awarded to William Lipscomb, Scholar of Corpus Christi College, for his *Beneficial Effects of Inoculation.* Two years later, though, inoculation was banned in the city by the vice chancellor and the mayor, although the practice remained legal until 1840, by which time it had, however, been largely superseded by the much safer vaccination.

St Ebbe's is the only parish to give many details of any interest between 1609 and 1832, with very high infant mortality generally. St Aldate's registers show smallpox outbreaks in January and February 1816, with two deaths and again in October and November the following year, with eleven fatalities, with seven deaths of the same disease in the latter half of 1828 and a single one the next January.

In 1832, on the eve of the first cholera outbreak, Oxford, although escaping the worst ravages of industrialization and urbanization, was no idyllic retreat. It continued to experience a whole range of diseases, some of them caused or exacerbated by unhealthy sites, crowded living conditions, inadequate water supply and sanitation, a shifting population and above all, a degree of poverty which made it impossible for those who wished to improve their living conditions to do so without considerable outside assistance. Furthermore, even within the affluent colleges, diseases were at work. Their task was made easier by those opportunities offered by a high concentration of communal living, factors which enabled diseases to spread rapidly among a population, the majority of whom had little previous exposure to the less sanitary aspects of urban life and therefore no opportunity of acquiring immunity.

Common sewers, formerly running streams, were by 1832 stagnant with filth and stench. In a letter dated 20 August Henry Roberts of St Thomas's complains that he was forced to leave his house at meal times because the stink put him off eating.

Parish pumps adjoined graveyards such as the survivor from St Mary the Virgin, which stands near the junction of St Mary's Entry and High Street.

From the seventeenth century technology had been available to provide a pure water supply but only to those who were willing and able to pay for it. It was not until it was glaringly obvious that many epidemic diseases were waterborne, and that the filthy lodgings of the poor were infecting middle and upper-class homes, that something had to be done.

In St Peter le Bailey a man named Jennings occupied a yard that contained a sty and tubs of pigswill which were crawling with maggots. In St Ebbe's there was a dog house and yard with putrefying horse flesh, a pig sty and all sorts of filth piled up.

When the beadle of St Thomas's parish inspected a house which had been the subject of a complaint to the Board of Health, he found pigsties, dung and other foulness including a cow's belly in a very bad state. Two pigs had died and been buried, it was assumed in the garden of the house.

A row of tenements in New Road, in St Peter le Bailey parish were scarcely fit for habitation because the soil from the privy emptied under the floorboards and rotted them so that they were dangerous to stand on.

In July 1832 Cherwell Street in St Clement's had filthy gutters, and an empty house recently occupied by prostitutes was very unwholesome. A privy overflowed creating a disgusting stench as did the neighbouring one.

Privies feature largely in reports, one of the worst being in Friar Street, St Ebbe's which spilt over behind four houses so that the excrement reached up to users' shoes and children could be seen at a pump, washing it from their legs. In York Place, St Clement's, one belonging to a butcher ran through the walls of neighbouring houses.

The fact that there were so many flagrant and persistent offenders highlights the weakness of the public health system in 1832. No legislation existed to enforce compliance with any directive issued.

Night-soil, a euphemism for human excrement, remained an issue throughout the nineteenth century with court cases involving spillages in the streets and roads.

Conditions in the next decade had improved little according to W.P. Ormerod in his seminal work *On the Sanatory Condition of Oxford* published in 1848 and relating to the years 1844, 1845, 1846. St Thomas's parish, for example:

> 'contains some of the worst habitations and the poorest inhabitants in Oxford. There are large, open drains and it is liable to flood. It is a matter of no surprise, that under these circumstances smallpox, scarlatina, diarrhoea and fever should have prevailed extensively... . In Hughes' Yard, a narrow court in Hythe Bridge, with rubbish heaps and only a small surface drain; this drain being quite insufficient and clogged up by a wooden pillar, which supports the building over the entrance to the court. The privy is for the whole court and is said not to have been cleaned out for two years. [p 24] Vaughan's Court is unpaved, but moderately open to the river at the end, which receives the contents of the privy. There are heaps of filth, and bad smells. One inhabitant complained much of the nuisance from a dog-kennel in the court. [There is] one lodging-house in the court,' [p25]...Nergrove Court: close and confined from a high wall opposite the houses; it is destitute of any drain of a useful kind and exceedingly filthy. There are pig-sties in front, and a most offensive bone-house is close to one end. There are ten houses and one privy, whilst a hole has been knocked through the floor of the court into an open ditch below.' [p26]

In the middle of the first cholera epidemic, the surgeon John Wood reported a high incidence of smallpox to the Board of Health in August 1832, together with his own dismay at the lack of vaccination among the city's poor. He volunteered to carry out vaccination without charge, as he had done on many previous occasions, but the board declined his offer, saying that it had no right to 'interfere'. [*Oxford Board of Health Minutes*, 22 August, 1832, MS Top Oxon c 272]

It is hardly surprising that Oxford's citizens, after learning to make the best of an assortment of lesser pestilences and having enjoyed nearly two centuries of freedom from 'the plague', found it difficult to accept the fact that they were being forced to endure what must have been seen as something very closely resembling its second coming.

Although epidemic diseases and in particular bubonic plague and cholera, caused reactions and revulsion which reverberate to this day, these diseases should not be allowed to assume unreal proportions within the structure of causes of death as a whole. It is important to remember the hundreds of less dramatic afflictions which killed our ancestors, many of them chronic rather than acute, but none the less exhausting, crippling and in the long run deadly.

Tuberculosis is the prime example of this process. This chronic recurring disease is caused by *mycobacterium tuberculosis* which is very similar to that responsible for leprosy. The pulmonary variety, the more usual throughout the nineteenth century, is often referred to as phthisis, which in the advanced stages, brings the cough, difficulty in breathing and coughing up of blood associated with tuberculosis.

Tuberculosis began to decline during the second half of the nineteenth century for reasons which remain unknown, although general improvements in personal hygiene, nutrition and living standards must have contributed. In Oxford, even during the cholera year of 1849, tuberculosis claimed more lives than any other disease, with seventy-seven fatalities, as opposed to cholera's seventy-five.

The year 1871 proved a bad one for smallpox. On 2 December *Jackson's* quoted the *Nuisances Removal Committee's Report* on smallpox returns as number of fresh cases sixteen, deaths, nil, total number receiving treatment thirty-one. Of the twenty-four cases in hospital, eighteen were convalescent. In other parts of the city there were two cases in St Thomas's, one in St Ebbe's, three in St Aldate's and one in St Clement's. The chairman of the committee ended his report with its recommendations concerning the funerals of smallpox victims. 'They strongly recommend that as few persons as possible attend such funerals, and that the corpses be in no cases taken into the churches or cemetery chapels.'

In the same edition of *Jackson's* is a letter to the editor:

> Sir, - Will you kindly allow me a small space in your Paper
> to contradict a malicious falsehood, circulated in the town,

doing much injury to my daughters in their business, stating that Mrs Wood died of small-pox. Dr Spencer having certified to her death being consumption, she being a great sufferer for twelve months.

I am, Sir, your obedient servant,
114 High-street, Oxford   HENRY WOOD

From 19 July 1879: a compositor named John Brownjohn, of Walton Street, was summoned for neglecting to have two of his children vaccinated. He pleaded guilty, stating that he objected to vaccination. The reason for this was that ten years before, he had joined a science class and obtained a government certificate, and his objection was based on what he had learnt on the course. The bench replied that their job was to administer the law, not make it, and he was fined five shillings and six shillings costs in each case. Brownjohn's was far from being a lone protest although his reasoning was unusual.

From *Jackson's* 16 January 1892:

'The epidemic in this city shows every sign, we regret to state, of a considerable increase, both in the number of persons attacked and deaths. Badly hit were the medical men of the city, the twelve members of the City Police, nine at the Post Office, fifteen at the GWR station, forty or fifty at the Clarendon Press and the Tramways Company. The Cutler Boulter Provident Dispensary were 2067, compared with 2031 the previous week, normally about 1100 to 1200, but fortunately no deaths occurred at the workhouse. Happily none of the medical staff at the Radcliffe Infirmary was affected.'

But *Jackson's* of 23 January 1892 read: 'In consequence of the prevalence of influenza in Oxford it is still considered desirable that the Christmas tree and entertainment for the patients in the Infirmary should be indefinitely postponed.'

From 15 April 1893: William Thomas Beesley of Speedwell Street was summoned because he 'unlawfully did expose' his daughter Emily while she was suffering from diphtheria, a bacterial infection that causes a thick covering to grow across the back of the throat and can lead to heart failure, paralysis and even death. Beesley 'also placed her in a public conveyance, without having given notice to the sanitary authority, in March 19th.' This was to take the child by cab to the Infectious Diseases Hospital. The cabman told Beesley that he should have sent for the carriage that was kept for this and he seemed very surprised. As the defendant did not realize the seriousness of what he had done, he was only fined two shillings with costs of one pound twelve shillings.

Chapter 11

Fatal Accidents

At the eyre of 1285 it was related how Beatrice, the daughter of Walter Hervey and Amy, the child of Thomas de Garford, were found burned to death in the cellar in the house of James the Spicer. There were no witnesses and no suspects. At the same session the jury heard how Robert the miller, William de Montibus's servant, was torn apart by a horse-powered mill wheel, and died immediately. The person who found him was not a suspect and had since died. The verdict was misadventure.

This obituary appeared in *Jackson's* of 16 September 1826:

> 'We have this week the melancholy task of announcing the death of Mr William Ward, second son of William Ward, Esq., banker and solicitor of this town; a gentleman uniting in himself all the amiable qualities of human nature. His death was occasioned by incautiously bathing in cold water after returning from a shooting excursion, which brought on an inflammation of the bowels, followed by a mortification, which terminated his life, in the 28th year of his age, to the universal grief of his friends and all those who had the pleasure of his acquaintance.'

Charles Blackstone, a scholar of Corpus Christi College had been 'exceedingly annoyed' by the presence of a rat in his rooms. In February 1849 he hired a loaded pistol from a gunsmith in order to shoot the animal but instead killed himself. The corpse, when viewed at the inquest, lay in its own room, with a 'countenance that still retained that calm and placid character peculiar to him in his life-time, and which distinctly told how instantaneous had been his death.'

A fellow student at Corpus stated that Blackstone had been 'very incautious with the pistol and had pointed it at the witness when it was loaded, and he had remarked to him that it was a foolish thing to do.' Another related how he had noticed a light in Blackstone's room just before one in the morning and had gone in to say goodnight. He found him on the sofa, apparently asleep. He shook the sofa then lifted Blackstone's right hand which was cold and which was holding the pistol. It was discovered that he was quite dead and there was blood on his shirt, coming from a wound on his left side. He agreed that the deceased had played very foolishly with the pistol when it was full cocked and had pointed at him as well.

The Rev Dr Norris, President of Corpus, stated that he had no reason whatsoever to think that this was a case of suicide 'for the deceased was in good odour throughout the whole College, from himself down to the junior member.' He had been an exemplary student and had hopes of a fellowship at the college in due time. Mr Martin, the surgeon, explained that the shot had penetrated the chest from front to back, passing through the left lung, and in its passage damaged the heart so that death would have been instant. He had extracted the bullet and produced it at the inquest. The jury's verdict as that 'the said Charles Blackstone caused his own death by accidentally discharging a loaded pistol, which he, as has been satisfactorily proved to the jury, had been in the habit of incautiously handling in his room.'

As surgeon Mr Symonds was leaving Christ Church in May 1868, after viewing the body of an undergraduate who had fallen from a roof, he was asked to go to Magdalen immediately. A student was discovered dying in the cloister and expired just after Symonds arrived. He was James Watson Barne of Exeter College who had been punting on the Cherwell with a fellow undergraduate, a Mr Gordon who was the only witness to the tragedy. Mr Barne had been shot by a bullet from a small pocket pistol used to shoot rats or birds on the riverbanks, 'a practice to which the Undergraduates are very prone, notwithstanding that a certain amount of danger ensues to those who may be on the banks at the time.' Mr Gordon steered the punt to Magdalen Bridge from where Mr Barne was carried to the cloisters where he cried, 'I am shot – I am dying – get me water.' The bullet had entered his right side between hip and chest and he died about half an hour afterwards around five o'clock.

The Rev C. Hammond, Fellow and tutor of Exeter College, drove down to the station and caught the five-thirty train to Devon in order to be the first to break the dreadful news to the deceased's widowed mother who lived in Tiverton. On the Thursday evening Mr Barne's body was 'removed in a shell by Messrs. Elliston and Cavell from Magdalen to Exeter College, where the inquest was appointed to be held.'

In September 1878 William Edward Robinson, a plumber aged 52, was working for his employer, Mr Hill of the High Street, in Tom Quad, Christ Church. When he stepped on a ladder on which a man named Harris from Jericho was standing, it snapped and he fell some twenty feet to the pavement below onto his left side. Both his thighs were broken and the left side of his head badly bruised; as his neck was broken it was thought that death was instantaneous. The verdict was 'Accidental death' and the inquest jury gave the fees to Mr Robinson's widow.

Thomas Cave, a fruiterer in his 50s who had business premises at 126 Walton Street lost his life in October 1893 in a most distressing way. One morning he went to a small dark cupboard in the back room of his premises. He swallowed what he took for Epsom Salts dissolved in water. Very soon afterwards he experienced vomiting and stomach pains and during the afternoon Dr Wilson was sent for. Mr Cave collapsed unconscious and nothing could be done to save him.

Because he had recently allowed betting to take place and had spent a few days in prison before his fine was paid, rumour had it that he had committed suicide. However, this proved completely untrue as there really was a packet of Epsom Salts in the dark cupboard, and it was at Cave's own request that Dr Wilson had been sent for. Public analyst, Mr Fisher, prepared a report on the contents of Mr Cave's stomach that he had vomited up. The poison was thought to be a vermin killer containing arsenic. The jury returned a verdict that death was caused by white arsenic taken accidentally by the deceased.

In November 1899 21-year-old Frederick Lacey, a miller of 2 Ferry Hinksey Road, became entangled in the machinery at Sheldon's Mill at Osney, then owned by a Mr James Archer. The deceased was said to be a steady man, used to being surrounded by machinery. A witness said that on the fatal morning he had heard a noise and seen a cloud of dust appear through the doorway. He immediately ran down to where Miller was and shouted at those below to stop the machinery which they did straight away. He could not see Miller for dust. He then made out the heel of his boot and found him hanging on the shaft with the belt round his arms; he noticed immediately that one of his legs had been torn off. The belt was cut and Miller released; he was still conscious and asked that something be put under his head and legs. They wrapped him in some sheets and sent him off to the infirmary, without going with him. He explained how the belt had come off and he had tried to replace it while the machinery was still in motion. This was a very unwise thing to do and doubtless caused the accident. Mr Winkfield, the surgeon, described how one leg was torn off and the other almost so. He had died from shock soon after reaching hospital. There was a good deal of discussion about what measures could and should be taken to make machinery safe. The jury 'added that they thought there ought to be a flange or guard attached to the wheel to prevent further accidents.' Frederick Miller's body was taken to his father's home and buried at Princes Risborough.

Animals could also be a cause of death. In May 1753 a child was bitten by a mad dog that was suspected to be rabid; the same week a total of seven people were bitten in the Gloucester Green area. They were all sent to Southampton to be dipped in the sea as salt water was then believed to be a cure for rabies. On 2 June the following year *Jackson's* reported how a 12-year-old boy from St Aldate's had suddenly been taken ill. The following day he was delirious, having bitten several people. As was the custom, he was sent off to Southampton for a salt dip. He had been bitten by a dog the previous Christmas with no apparent ill effects.

One evening in October 1885, as Thomas Baker of English's Row, St Aldate's, brought a boar from New Hinksey into the city. The animal, which was not previously known to be of a savage nature, attacked an elderly man named Richard Collett of South Hinksey and inflicted such serious injuries that he had to be taken to the infirmary where he died two days later. The inquest jury heard how the animal had rushed at several people who managed to beat it off and then went for Mr Collett and knocked him over. He received three large wounds, two on the buttock and one on the back of the thigh. He had died from shock and loss of blood. After a verdict of 'Accidental death' had been returned, the coroner 'made some apt remarks as to the custom of taking such animals about the streets without being under proper control.'

A leisurely drive through the city's ancient streets in one's carriage or a longer jaunt to one of the outlying villages sounds ideal but in practice it could prove nothing of the kind. There are numerous accounts of horses bolting, shying, throwing their riders, treading on people and otherwise behaving dangerously. They were frequently involved in lethal accidents. Thomas Bowell had taken his daughter to the Radcliffe

Infirmary in November 1834, and then went across to the Royal Oak opposite where he had left his horse and cart. He was standing to one side, adjusting the harness when the horse suddenly reared up and ran off with the cart, knocking Mr Bowell down. He landed on his head and was taken straight back to the infirmary where everything possible was done for him. However, he died a few days later from concussion of the brain.

One evening in May 1849 'an accident occurred near Magdalen Bridge, affording another proof how soon, even from a thoughtless act, the life of a fellow creature may be sacrificed.' A young man aged about 18 named Thomas Meyers, who worked for Ward and Company coal merchants, was driving two empty carts fastened together across Magdalen Bridge when Charles Hamilton, a Bluecoat boy, tried to clamber into the second one. In order to stop him, Meyers threw a small piece of coal at the lad and in doing so overbalanced and fell out of the cart; the wheels passed over his head and killed him immediately. He was taken to the Flying Horse where an inquest was held on his body. The coroner lectured Hamilton on his stupid act 'which had been the means of hurrying a fellow creature, without a moment's notice, into the presence of his Maker, and expressed a hope that this melancholy affair would have a salutary effect on his conduct through life.'

Richard Simms, who was almost blind, was coming back from Summertown and walking in the middle of the road late one night in September 1855 when he was knocked over. He was about 150 yards from the Horse and Jockey public house when he was hit by a dog-cart driven by Lord Dillon. Dillon pulled up immediately and finding that Simms was badly injured, drove back to the Horse and Jockey to get help. Some passers-by helped the injured man onto the pavement. Lord Dillon drove to the city police station only to find it closed but soon afterwards came across one of the university police and drove him back in the dog-cart to where the accident had taken place. He then ordered Simms to be taken to the Radcliffe Infirmary where he would be taken care of and gave the policeman a half-sovereign to thank the men who had come to his assistance. When Simms was picked up he was unconscious and stayed that way for another two days, when he died.

In July 1882 Mr John Edward Henderson, Fellow and estates bursar of Magdalen College died of injuries received when a horse ran away. Mr Henderson was pulling a poor woman out of its way as it was dashing up George Street when he was himself knocked down. He received a compound fracture of the right leg in addition to internal injuries. Leading medical men in the city were consulted and Mr Henderson appeared to be making satisfactory progress when things took a decided turn for the worse and he died. He had been 'a great favourite among all classes in Oxford and his untimely death had been the subject of general commiseration.'

A 40-year-old butcher named Isaac Simmons of Cranham Street, met his death in September 1887 when his pony cart collided with a timber wagon in Walton Street. After the accident the deceased was picked up and carried off to the Radcliffe Infirmary where, after laying there unconscious for some hours, he died. The inquest heard that Simmons had been driving along Walton Street and attempted to push between the timber wagon which was turning into a yard and a hand-cart that was parked by the side of the pavement. As he did so, his wheel caught against that of the timber wagon and he was thrown out onto his head.

From 17 December 1887: the 65-year-old wife of an old and respected Oxford tradesman in the High Street, was killed in a carriage accident at the top of the Banbury Road. Mr Theophilus Carter, an upholsterer was taking his wife for a drive and they were on their way to Kidlington when just past Sunnymeade their horse shied at another horse and bolted across the road. The carriage overturned, pitching Mrs Carter head first onto the footpath. She never spoke or moved again and it is certain that the fall fractured the base of her skull. She was still breathing when she was taken to the Radcliffe Infirmary but was found to be dead on arrival. Her body was then removed to her home in the High Street. This was the same Mr and Mrs Carter whose son had committed suicide in his bedroom just before Christmas 1876.

About two-thirty one Tuesday afternoon in May 1890, Lieutenant Levett-Scrivener, bursar of Keble College, and his wife were riding on horseback. They were near the railway bridge when the lady's horse was startled 'by the whistling and escape of steam of an engine' and becoming restive started off at a canter. It suddenly swerved to the left, mounted the pavement, slipped and fell, throwing Mrs Levett-Scrivener onto the roadway. She landed on her head and the horse rolled onto her. She was taken, bleeding and unconscious, to the house of a Mr Bell where she was given every attention until the horse ambulance was summoned and she was carried to Dr Sankey's home in St Giles, and then to her home at 10 Canterbury Road. She never spoke after the accident, indeed she never regained consciousness and died about four o'clock. She had sustained a fracture of the skull, and there was a large bruise over her left eye. She was only 25 years old and left a family of young children.

Fred Shurmer aged 43, of 31 Boulter Street, St Clement's, was killed while trying to stop a runaway cab-horse on the evening of Boxing Day 1899. The horse had run off with a carriage in tow near Magdalen Bridge, unwisely running straight to the animal's head rather than at the side or a little behind it. He was knocked over and very badly injured then taken to the infirmary where he died from internal injuries before the operation planned to save his life had started. Mr Shurmer, who left a widow and a large family of children, had been a servant at St Edmund Hall.

The driver of the four-wheeler, Henry Miller of Percy Street, deposed that he was taking a party from Headington to the Iffley Road when he stopped at the bottom of Headington Hill as he had not proper control of the horse and so he got down to adjust the reins. As he was getting back onto the driving seat, the horse lunged forward and he was knocked over. The horse then bolted in the direction of Magdalen Bridge. Both Miller and a witness who saw Miller adjust the reins said that he was perfectly sober. A post mortem showed that Shurmer had a ruptured bladder which extended about four inches and it was unlikely that an operation would have saved his life. As there were no witnesses to the accident itself, a verdict of 'Accidental death' was returned and the jury donated their fees to the widow.

About midday one May day in 1886 an elderly man named Frederick Sammons from Plantation Road, was knocked down and killed by a two-horse tram as he tried to cross the road in front of it. Mr Sammons was very deaf and was not aware of how close the tram was, nor did he hear the driver's shouts until it was too late although the brakes were put on hard. 'When the poor old man was knocked down by the pole under the hoofs of the horses, they were startled, and no stoppage could be effected until both the front and rear wheels had passed over him. The immediate cause of death was doubtless fracture of the skull, caused by one or both of the horses trampling on him, his head being so visibly cut that it was not deemed necessary to call medical testimony to depose to the extent of the injuries.' Mr Sammons was still alive when picked up but died in St John's Road, now St Bernard's Road, while being taken to the Radcliffe Infirmary.

Eli Burchell, guard on the London to Manchester goods train that arrived in Oxford about two-thirty-four in the morning, met with a fatal accident in November 1862. The train had stopped near the West Midlands goods depot to unload and move wagons and the engine and carriages were detached. Burchell was standing with his back to the engine, talking to another employee, when he was knocked down by a parcel van that passed right over him, breaking his right arm and cutting away one of his calves, which opened up a vein and killed him within four hours of his being admitted to the infirmary.

Plate-layer's labourer, Joseph Green, aged 28 of South Street, Osney, was knocked down by an engine at the London and North Western Railway Station in March 1894. It was necessary to amputate his leg but 'the poor fellow never having rallied from the shock' died. His widow told how she had heard that her husband had been involved in an accident and went up to the infirmary where she sat with him all night. He was conscious and told her that in trying to get out of the way of the engine he turned and was hit. The train driver had blown his whistle to alert Green. A witness helped to move him and noticed that his leg was bleeding. Despite this Green tried to walk as he did not think that his leg was broken. The witness and a mate put Green onto a trolley and took him to the station and then to the infirmary. When asked why he had taken the fatal step, Green replied that he thought that the train was on the other set of rails. The house surgeon at the infirmary stated that the deceased had an extensive lacerated wound on the left leg and thigh, involving the knee joint and a fracture of one of the bones in the leg. When questioned he confirmed that Green would have had better chances of recovery after an amputation than if he had not had one.

Fatal falls were also only too common in Oxford. An inquest held on 3 December 1300 heard that Roger de Metham, a 16-year-old clerk, died in St Mildred's parish. He had gone to Bole Hall to meet friends in an upstairs room where he sat by a window which gave way, so that he fell to the ground and was killed.

From 5 January 1301: Robert de Honniton, clerk, died after lingering since 31 December when he had climbed up the tower of St Michael's church intending to help ring the bells but fell out of an opening and, landing on his right side, received so much damage that by the time he died his right side was badly swollen and blackened.

It is to be hoped that what happened to Francis Bayley of Christ Church in July 1713 was unique. He had been in the habit of going missing for a day or two so his disappearance one Monday evening did not cause alarm. It was not until the Thursday that he was missed, when someone remembered seeing him in his nightgown. When a search was finally organized, the unfortunate youth was discovered in the college 'house of office' or privy, completely smothered having leant back too far and fallen into the pit below the lavatory. Canon Stratford noted, belatedly, that he had often complained that the seats were too large and had no backs. Bayley must have died slowly and painfully. Another student had entered the privy around eleven on the Monday night but had been scared away by groans coming from the building. Another member of college had heard a noise a good hour later but assumed that someone was being sick in Bear Lane, while another, who at least ventured in, thought it was just a dog.

From 30 June 1827: Henry Perkins, gentleman commoner of New College was leaving a party at St John's College when on his way down a staircase, his foot slipped and he fell to the bottom, dislocating his neck. He was the son of an eminent London brewer who, with his family, had taken lodgings in Oxford and were just setting out when 'the melancholy intelligence was communicated.' On the advice of Mr Tuckwell, surgeon, the jury returned a verdict 'that the deceased died of apoplexy, occasioned by the hurt he received in the fall.'

From 16 May 1840: one Tuesday morning, the Rev G. Grantham, senior Fellow and bursar of Magdalen College had a fatal accident. He occupied a set of rooms on the second floor of the New Building which overlooks the college deer park. The previous evening, he had lain back on his sofa and fallen asleep for quite a while until he was woken up by an unpleasant smell from a candle that had burnt out. He then went over to the window and stood on a chair to open it. Unfortunately, the wood had recently been varnished and it needed quite an amount of strength to force the sash open. It must have suddenly given way and the Rev Grantham lost his balance and fell through.

This must have happened after two in the morning as two members of the college who were sitting up reading in the rooms beneath and would have heard the fall, did not go to bed until then. About six o'clock a college servant doing his rounds of the gentlemen's rooms noticed the deer gathered around in a strange way and when he went to see why, he found the dead body. Medical assistance was sent for but it was apparent that 'the vital spark had been extinct for two or three hours.' Death would have been 'almost instantaneous, for on examination it appeared that there was a violent concussion of the brain, a bursting of some of the vessels in the head, besides several of the ribs being broken.' G.V. Cox, the university coroner, returned a verdict of accidental death.

From 10 March 1849: The dead body of John Key, a first-term student of Oriel College, was found in the south-east corner of the front quadrangle near the chapel door and close to the hall stairs. From the injuries that he had sustained it was obvious that the deceased had fallen from the top floor of the college, a height of about forty feet. Cox, held an inquest in the hall with a jury composed of matriculated citizens.

Mr Martin, surgeon, deposed that he had been called to Oriel about quarter to seven that morning where he found the body of Mr Key. He lay on his stomach, his face turned to the left. His right arm and wrist were fractured, the left shoulder dislocated. Blood was coming from his mouth. Death would have been instantaneous due to concussion of the brain.

A fellow student, H.M. Maughan, explained how, between three and four that morning he had heard a scuffling noise. Then Key came to his room and tried the locked door. He sounded 'furious with rage' but calmed down after a few minutes' whispered conversation. Maughan told him to go back to his own rooms and thought that he had done so. Key returned, saying that his sitting-room door was locked so Maughan told him to get into his room through the window over the staircase door, giving him a chair and a candle to do so. He did not seem drunk, just still very angry. He intended to gain access to the leads, saying that he was a great climber. When Maughan refused to hand over the key he demanded a coal hammer to break down the door.

T.A. Cox, another undergraduate, stated that Key had been too drunk to look after himself and several undergraduates had tried to settle him down. They were unable to undress him and when they tried to fasten his door he prevented them from doing so by thrusting his arms in the way. Eventually they barricaded him in with a sofa and tables and left, by which time he had quietened down; they then locked his outer door. The jury decided 'that the said John Key having, as it appears to the Jury, got out on the roof, did accidently fall over the parapet, and was killed by the fall.'

FATAL ACCIDENTS

From 16 May 1868: Peckwater Quad at Christ Church was the scene of 'the violent and sudden death of Mr Robert Marriott, one of the most popular junior members of that establishment. The deceased was a very spirited and daring young fellow…cheery and adventurous.' He was very fond of climbing, including scaling the outside of various college buildings, both in the High Street and going from room to room at Christ Church. It was unclear about what went wrong on this last, fatal climb but it is likely that crumbling stone work played its part. Marriott had already made an unsuccessful attempt to climb up to where he had fallen from and he had stated his intention to try again. This ruled out any suggestion of sleepwalking.

The coroner and his jury viewed the body of 'a fine young man, apparently about 20 years of age. The neck was badly injured, if not dislocated and the head fractured on both its sides.' The deceased was due to play in a rugby match that was postponed because of the tragedy and the Christ Church cricket ground was closed for a day as a mark of respect and the college eight did not turn out for its usual practice. The flags as well as those of Exeter College, were flown at half mast.

From 5 February: a dreadful accident took place at the prison involving a warder called Henry Bell, of 21 Percy Street, Iffley Road. He had been taken on as a temporary warder for about six weeks and on the day in question was superintending five prisoners who were busy in one of the yards moving old timbers which had come from the older section of the gaol in the course of a building alteration. In this yard was an area about eight feet deep and the same wide, and the deceased was walking along the edge of this when he suddenly fell from the coping. In doing so he must have turned almost a complete somersault and fallen on his head, smashing the top of his skull.

When picked up he was unconscious and died shortly afterwards. Nothing could be done for him apart from making him as comfortable as possible during his last moments. Blood came frothing from his mouth and he was not able to explain what had happened. Not surprisingly his widow was deeply distressed and shocked; the couple had six young children.

The coroner stressed that it was most important that the prisoners should be absolved of any blame whatsoever in the accident. The jury returned a verdict of 'Accidental death' and gave their fees to the widow of the deceased.

From 17 September 1892: Annie Breakspear aged 52 had gone to St Giles's Fair and was riding on a steam roundabout that was going at great speed when she suffered a dreadful accident. She was riding on one of the outside horses when she fell off, doubtless accidentally. She had fallen some seven or eight feet and the back of her head hit the ground. When she was picked up she was unconscious and remained so for the further thirty-four hours that she lived.

It was established that she was unmarried and had worked at Hyde's clothing factory. She had been in good health and it was thought that her eyesight was not impaired in any way that might have caused her fall. It was then stated that the deceased had been holding a neighbour's child on the horse when they fell off together. Fortunately, the little girl's fall was broken when she landed on Miss Breakspear's leg. The child said that it was by trying to save her from falling that the deceased lost her balance. The verdict was that she died from a fractured skull.

Chapter 12

Drownings

Drownings have been so common in Oxford and its environs that they warrant a separate section. Perhaps this is not surprising in view of the large number of water courses throughout the town, 'more in number than your eyelashes', as Keats wrote in a letter to a friend.

The 1285 eyre contains several examples, such as how a clerk named Alexander Comyn drowned in the River Cherwell and nobody else was suspected of being involved. An unnamed clerk took the corpse to the church of Holy Cross in Holywell. Bailiff Walter de Chawsey, on the orders of nobleman Bogo de Clare, tried unsuccessfully to prevent the coroner viewing the body or holding an inquest. Walter was present at the inquest and unable to deny what had happened and was therefore sent to gaol.

Nicholas le Forc, another clerk, drowned in the River Thames. Afterwards Andrew le Forc, John Bere and Geoffrey Fresel came and carried him to the church of St Michael at North Gate where they had him buried without the coroner seeing the body so they were fined. Nobody was suspected of harming Nicholas and a verdict of accidental death was given.

The Coroner's Roll of John of Osney, 1297-1301 [Oxfordshire History Centre, reference P6/1L/1] includes the following: on 8 December 1298, he heard how Isolda, daughter of William Kyng, aged 7 ½ was found drowned near the mill under Oxford Castle, having fallen in when going home by night, presumably by herself.

On 19 Feb 1298/9, the inquest concerned Simon de Stodley who had been found dead in the Thames by Hythe Bridge in St Thomas's parish having fallen in one night while drunk. Similarly, on 19 March 1298/9 Richard Hilde of Shifford was found dead by the same bridge by his wife Juliana. Apparently he had been sailing on the river when drunk, and when near the bridge at Godstow his boat had overturned and he had drowned. The enquiry on 24 August 1299 also sounds quite modern: Adam de la Wyke was found dead at la Wyke, a hamlet near Binsey by his wife Alice, after he had fallen in a ditch and drowned while trying to get home one night from the inn.

On 2 August 1300, William de Bangor, an Irish clerk was found dead near a dam belonging to Osney Abbey by Richard de Hayle, who raised the hue. William had no marks on his body and the jury concluded he had drowned while trying to bathe in the River Thames. The verdict was death by misadventure.

On 7 December 1301, the body of John de Neushom, a clerk and a schoolmaster, was dragged from the River Cherwell where he had been found by his wife Isabella. The inquest heard that after lunch on a previous day he had gone off in search of switches to use for punishing his pupils. Having climbed up a willow tree near a millpond to cut off suitable branches, John fell in the water and drowned.

A section of the northern side of Magdalen Bridge fell down in February 1665 and a boy was killed when he fell into the water, drowned, and was carried off to the weir.

About five in the afternoon of 10 May 1666 great claps of thunder were heard in the city and these were followed by torrential rain. Shortly before the storm two members of Wadham College had set out in a boat from Medley without a waterman and had just pushed off from the riverbank to return to Oxford. They were standing near the bow when they were thrown out of the boat and into the water by a flash of lightning. They were fished out after only a minute or so but one of them, Samuel Mashbourne, was seen to be stone dead. His friend was stuck by his feet in the mud and unable to move, so stunned that he could not remember anything about what had happened to them. He was pulled out and put into a warm bed but had not completely recovered by the following night.

About six o'clock one July morning in 1830, John Johnson the assistant and Robert Rouse, the shop boy of John Hitchcock, a perfumer in the Cornmarket, went to bathe at Medley Lock. Johnson, who was an expert swimmer, suggested taking the boy on his shoulders and swimming with him through the lock. At first Rouse refused but then climbed onto Johnson who swam off. Then, according to 'an intelligent boy who was present', the lad became too heavy and weighed his friend down in the water. Rouse became upset and wanted to go back but he could not and soon Johnson 'sunk to rise no more.' The boy tried to make his way back to the riverbank but as he could not swim he sank within a few yards. Apart from the young boy and one other there were no witnesses and as neither of these could swim either, both lives were lost. The coroner issued a warning against the practice only too common locally, of young men carrying smaller ones on their backs in deep water. The unfortunate persons drowned, the elder aged around 19, the younger not yet 15, were both 'remarkably steady and attentive to the interest of their employer.'

William Robert Cookson of University College, who had only just matriculated, was rowing in an outrigger on the Isis in November 1859 when he was seized with an epileptic fit, to which he was subject. He fell into the water and drowned before anyone could help him despite there being several people in the vicinity, both on the towpath and on the river. The surgeon George Hitchings was sent for and found the body lying in a punt while attempts at resuscitation were still being attempted. It was however, clear that this would be useless as the face was badly discoloured which might have indicated that the young man had had a fit. Mr Cookson, who came from Newcastle upon Tyne, was buried in Holywell Cemetery.

An undergraduate at Keble College lost his life in February 1876 when the boat in which he was in turned over near Magdalen College Water Walks. Sidney Saunders, aged about 20, went off in a canoe with a friend; neither of the young men could swim. When near the King's Mill where the water was overhung with trees, the friend became entangled in low branches and the canoe overturned. Almost immediately the friend was rescued but Saunders was seen to be in difficulties. Despite the efforts of William Morris, a member of New College to save him, he sank below the water. Drags were used but there were so many roots muddying the water that it was impossible for divers to see more than a few inches ahead of them and the body was recovered some distance away nearly an hour later. The body was taken to the herbarium of the Botanic Garden and the inquest jury made up of members of the university and matriculated tradesmen. It was pointed out that at Eton, Radley and Cambridge, young men were not permitted to take out boats if they were unable to swim.

Sidney Harriss, an apprentice of R.W. Bell, draper of Park End Street, was one of a group from Commercial Road Baptist Chapel that went on the river to Nuneham on the *British Queen* in August 1879. He had returned in a small boat with two ladies and two other young men. They landed safely then Harriss turned back to fetch something that he had left and walked off the end of the raft into the river in the darkness. He was unable to swim and although two or three people were close by, he was never seen to come to the surface and the rapid current must have carried him away immediately. A search was made using punt poles but it was not for three-quarters of an hour that he was found caught up in a bed of weeds about twenty yards away.

One Friday afternoon in March 1882 William Morris-Jones, a member of Jesus College died when his boat was overturned. With two other members of the college he started to row to Sandford; when reaching Iffley Lock, the boat went into the stream leading to the mill and overturned. Morris-Jones was quickly swept away and drowned and the boat smashed against the sluices. The body was recovered the following day some 200 yards from where the accident happened. An inquest was held at Jesus College the same evening. The jury recommended that the post bearing the word 'Danger' currently in the middle of the river, should be moved higher up the river onto the bank and further from the sluices.

On the Monday morning the deceased's body was taken to the Great Western Railway Station, followed by the Principal of Jesus, and all the members of the college, to be taken to Bangor where the funeral took place.

In April 1882 the body of woman was found in the Isis near Long Bridges. The face was badly disfigured and bloated; it was first suspected that foul play had been involved but closer investigation showed that the facial marks were due to decomposition. The body was taken to the Weirs Inn where it was identified as Elizabeth Heydon who had not been seen since the University Boat Race. This was done by two women who knew her by a mole on the chest, a missing tooth and the finding of a button-hook and some threepenny pieces in the dress pocket which the deceased was known to carry for luck. However, Mr Ballard the surgeon pointed out that there was no mole in the place indicated and that the teeth were intact at which the women declared that they were now equally sure that it was not Elizabeth Heydon after all.

It was then decided that the corpse was that of Sophia Facer aged 18, of James Street, Iffley Road who shortly beforehand had taken a job as a barmaid at a London hotel and had gone to watch the boat race. Soon afterwards she left the hotel, got into a cab and was not seen alive again. The coroner said there was no evidence to show how the deceased came to be in the water; there was no evidence of foul play and the verdict was therefore 'Found drowned'.

Between eight and nine on a Wednesday morning in December 1885, a large section of the central arch of the bridge over the Thames at Osney collapsed. Rumours abounded that several people had been swept away by the current and drowned but fortunately these proved to be untrue. It is unclear how many people were in fact on the bridge when it fell in but it was thought that four were thrown into the water of whom at least one was rescued by a Mr Greenaway of Mill Street who jumped in to help them. Four or five hats were certainly recovered from the river but the loss was believed to be confined to one child, whose surname was Miles, swept away by the current despite Mr Greenaway's gallant attempts to reach her. At the time of writing the report her body had not been recovered. Thankfully, there were several narrow escapes.

In June 1889 'a most deplorable fatality' took place on the Isis between Osney and Folly Bridge, the victim having 'with great gallantry' rescued 9-year-old Christopher Green and Thomas Hazell aged 10 who had fallen into the river while fishing. Edgar George Wilson, 21, of 14 Abbey Road, was the son of the Rev George Wilson, minister of the Commercial Road Baptist Chapel. Wilson was walking along the towpath when he saw the boys in difficulties. He appears to have jumped into the river fully clothed, despite the fact that he could not swim. The youngsters managed to get onto the bank but tragically Edgar was drowned, one reason being suggested that his arm had tangled up with the boys' fishing lines.

A memorial was erected on the ground donated by University College at a cost of twenty-two pounds collected by subscription from about 2,000 Oxford residents. About 200 people came to the unveiling on 7 November 1889.

An enquiry was held on 31 January 1891 by the coroner into the death of a schoolboy Albert Lovegrove aged 11, son of Frederick Lovegrove a college servant living in Circus Street. Albert, together with two school friends had left school at midday and gone down to the river in Christ Church Meadow. They clambered onto a block of ice that immediately tipped up and all three boys were thrown into the water. Two of the boys were rescued but tragically, Albert was drowned. Mr Lovegrove told the court that Albert should have come home for lunch around twelve-thirty. A boy called William Allnutt came to the Lovegroves' house to say that their son had walked onto the ice and could not be found. The father went down to the river and stayed there until his son's body was taken out of the water by the university waterman, William Talboys. The verdict was accidental death.

A gravestone in Holywell cemetery has an inscription that tells a tragic story:

LEWIS THEODORE AGED 4 YEARS & 2 MONTHS

ONLY CHILD OF GILES THEODORE & SOPHIA MARGARETTA PILCHER

ELIZABETH SIBLEY AGED 22 YEARS HIS DEVOTED NURSE

HEREWITH WAS IN JESUS CHRIST THE SAME YESTERDAY TODAY & FOR EVER

DROWNED TOGETHER NEAR MEDLEY WEIR MAY 31ST 1893

Ellen Louisa Goodall aged 18, of the Civet Cat in Cornmarket Street, was drowned when the boat in which she was sailing capsized in May 1893, just before ten o'clock on a bright moonlit night. The deceased was in a boat with her sister and two male friends. The party had come from Iffley and noticed the steamer *Alesha* moored opposite the Isis Tavern. One of the men, who appeared as a witness, asked the engineer if they could fasten their boat for a tow and gave him the head rope which he tied to the steamer's stern bar. When they passed between Weirs Bridge and The Kidneys, the boat started to swerve because the rope was a little too long and this caused the accident. The boat began to take in water slowly and then very fast. The young man cut the rope and released the boat from the swell of the steamer but by that time the boat was full of water and started to sink. He went to the stern to try to rescue the ladies but soon all four were in the river. They would have been all right had the boat not turned over and the third time this happened Miss Goodall was lost. He caught hold of her and got her to hold his arm with one hand and the boat with the other but she went under into about eleven feet of water and did not rise again to the surface. The third time that the boat turned over was due to the younger sister clutching at its sides.

Finally a man called Green, who was the mate on the steamer, answered their cries for help and swam out to take hold of the boat and bring it to the bank. He was joined by a university waterman from the *Alaska* that was coming from Iffley. By the time the body was discovered Miss Goodall was stone dead. After returning a verdict of 'accidentally drowned' the jury added a rider that the practice of attaching small boats to steamers should be discouraged.

Miss Goodall's funeral took place in Holywell Cemetery; the inscription on the coffin read: 'NELLIE LOUISA GOODALL, died 27th April, 1893, aged 18 years.'

One morning, in February 1899 Charles Turner, an employee of the Weirs paper mill saw something in the pool. He saw that it was the body of a woman 'in a remarkable condition'. The body was taken from the water to the mortuary, where it was seen to resemble 'a dilapidated statue. Decomposition appears to have been arrested at an early stage by petrifaction, the flesh becoming stone-like by the action of lime in the water. There is a hole in the stomach, some of the fingers are missing, and the features are undistinguishable. The deceased, who was apparently about five feet six inches in height, was wearing a wedding ring, which was much worn and points to the fact that she was of middle age. Among the few shreds of clothing which remain, a piece of black astrakhan round the neck can be seen, and this may help in identification.' The police officer who dealt with the case added that there was also a black stocking on the right leg and a glove hanging by a button from the right hand. Nearly all the hair had been washed away.

Dr Turrell and the jury saw the body and the doctor judged that it had been in the water some three or four months. He suggested further attempts at identification might include looking for broken limbs or gold fillings.

From 30 June 1900: an inquest was held before the coroner on the body of Margaret Serey aged 35, wife of Arthur Serey, a labourer of Paradise Place. She was found drowned in the Old River, near Hythe Bridge Street, early one morning. The coroner told the jury that what 'he had to unfold to them was a somewhat sad and ghastly one,' but that their decision should be relatively simple. He believed that the woman was an 'unfortunate' or prostitute, who had left her home on the Saturday night around ten-thirty or eleven, 'doubtless for immoral purposes'. Several witnesses told how they had seen her that night and that she was certainly in a drunken state. She made her way along the towpath leading from Hythe Bridge between the river and the canal. When she did not come back, her husband went to look for her and the following morning she was found dead in the river. There was nothing to show how she had got into the river, so the proper verdict would be the usual 'Found drowned'. The jury, on deliberation, returned that verdict and the inquest finished.

What is so difficult to understand is how this depressingly long list was allowed to happen. Many of the reports contain the information that the deceased was unable to swim. From time to time meetings were held about introducing safety measures; indeed the baths in Bath Street, St Clement's were opened in 1827, not for hygienic reasons but to curb the number of fatalities. Life-saving equipment was installed at advertised points along the riverbank and towpaths but this does beg the question why young people were not taught to swim as a matter of course, and why boating businesses were allowed to hire craft out to those clearly incapable of using them safely.

Chapter 13

Suicides

Doing away with oneself became a crime in English common law in the middle of the thirteenth century but according to the Church it had long been a mortal sin. For a death to be declared *felo de se*, the old legal term for suicide, it first had to be proved that the deceased was in his or her right mind at the time.

If the verdict was suicide a Christian burial was forbidden and at night the corpse was taken to a crossroads and tossed into a hole, sometimes with a wooden stake pinning it down. No form of religious service, or even a mourner, was allowed. The punishment extended to the deceased's family whose possessions were forfeited to the Crown until 1822. The Burial of Suicide Act 1823 meant that a suicide could be interred in a churchyard but only between the hours of nine and midnight, with a clergyman in attendance but still without rites. The Interments (*Felo de se*) Act of 1882 permitted burial at any hour and with the normal rites.

As with assaults and murders, stabbing was a popular method of dispatching oneself. On 7 June 1670, Richard Berry, chaplain of Christ Church, called 'a simple hot-headed coxcomb' by Wood, out of his head with drink, or besotted with a pedlar named Bess Faulkner, or else 'overcharged with spring blood', like someone suffering from any of these afflictions, stabbed himself with a knife in his room in the Chaplain's Quadrangle at Christ Church about six o'clock in the morning. After weltering in his own blood for some time, he happened to be saved by his bed-maker who, on seeing what he had done and the room full of blood sent for a surgeon who dressed his wounds. After this behaviour, he was packed off to Ireland by the college where he 'got into some cathedral' to be a chaplain or minor canon.

After dinner on 8 August 1676 Richard Imming, a former scholar of Corpus Christi College, killed himself with a rapier on the riverbank near Osney Mill. His burial in St Thomas's churchyard on the north side of the chancel, was paid for by an apothecary named John Haselwood who had married Imming's sister, who had also died mad. Wood calls Imming a melancholy man.

From 30 December 1826: an inquest was taken at the Rising Sun in St Ebbe's parish on the body of Edwin Serle, a very steady young man, recently employed by a tailor named Purbrick. Serle had cut his throat 'in a most dreadful manner, nearly severing his head from the body. There is every reason to believe that this unfortunate young man took off his coat, waistcoat, and neck cloth and stood before a looking glass to perpetrate the dreadful act; he afterwards went towards the staircase, where he fell from loss of blood, and was found by a neighbour a most shocking spectacle.' The wound was described as being about six inches in length and deep enough to 'have completely divided the windpipe and the passage leading to the stomach behind; and the jugular vein on each side, and carotid artery on the right side were both severed; the wound inflicted was the cause of his death.'

The jury heard that nothing out of the ordinary had been noticed about Serle's behaviour in the days immediately before the tragedy and 'after a very short deliberation unanimously returned a verdict of – *Felo de se*; and the Coroner issued his warrant for the burial between the hours of 9 and 12, as directed by the Act of 4th George IV.'

From 20 May 1870: a jury representing both Town and Gown was told about the distressing suicide of Favour James Gregg of Balliol College on Port Meadow. A friend stated that he had been very depressed because his mother had been confined in an asylum. A witness described how he had been crossing Port Meadow with a horse and cart when he noticed black under a hedge. On looking closer he saw that it was a man lying on his side. He called out, 'Halloa, governor; what's the game now?' He got no reply, the man merely drawing up his legs. 'I went over to his side,' he continued, 'I saw his eyes work. He raised his head a little way, and the blood began gulping out.' The witness then drove to Wolvercote Police Station and the man was taken by cart to the Radcliffe Infirmary. 'He tried to speak but there was only a rattling in his throat. There was a wonderful lot of blood about where he lay.' A razor covered in blood was found at the scene. Gregg later died at the infirmary.

From 16 January 1886: an inquest was held in the infirmary on an agricultural labourer, William Lockton, aged 67, who had committed suicide there. Lockton, from nearby Elsfield, had been an inmate of the Littlemore lunatic asylum, 'but of course' says *Jackson's,* 'he was not supposed to be insane, or he would not have been admitted to that Infirmary.'

William Lockton's daughter, who identified the body, said that he had been in poor health for some time and unable to work due to failing eyesight, the reason why he was in the infirmary. Mr Redman, a house surgeon, stated that the deceased had cataracts on both eyes and in the summer had undergone an unsuccessful operation. He had been depressed but not worryingly so. On the morning that he was due to be discharged, the surgeon was called to see Lockton and found him quite dead. There were several small cuts or dashes in the skin of his throat which were not deep enough to kill him, but on looking further down, Redman 'found the bowels exposed, and there was a large wound in the abdominal wall sufficient to cause death.' Not surprisingly there was a large amount of blood in the bed. A pocket knife, about four inches long and with a pointed blade was found by his side. The corpse's hands were bloody and Redman believed that nobody else would have inflicted the wound. The jury returned a verdict that he had given himself a mortal wound with a pocket knife while of an unsound mind.

From 28 June 1890: an inquest was held at a house in Wellington Square on the body of Mrs Anne Petch, 54 years of age, who committed suicide by cutting her throat with a table knife, early one morning. The deceased was the widow of the Rev George Petch, Vicar of Oddington, since whose death she had lived in Oxford.

Her son-in-law the Rev Harry Ketchley of the same address, deposed that the deceased was his mother-in-law, and there had seemed nothing unusual when she had gone to bed the previous night.

The following morning, her daughter remarked that it was unusual that Mrs Petch had not called them and so went to her room. She gave a shriek and on joining her he saw the deceased lying on her side in the bed, still in her nightdress, with a large wound on her throat and surrounded by a lot of blood. He was certain that she was dead; the body was still just warm and rigor mortis had set in. He noticed two ordinary table knives on the bed, one splashed with blood.

Mrs Petch had been having medical attention for some time as she had been suffering from dizzy spells and a spinning head and been in low spirits as there was little hope of her health improving. This had made her in a very morbid state. The verdict was that 'the deceased committed suicide while of an unsound state of mind.'

Hanging did not require any accessories but it did require privacy and some forward planning. On 2 February 1674 Martin Roseenstan, a Dane staying at the house of Mrs Mumford near the Sheldonian Theatre, hanged himself about four or five in the morning. He had got up about four o'clock on the fateful morning, made up the fire, taken off his shirt and gone downstairs naked carrying his coat, leggings, hose and shoes. Taking up a candle, he went to the privy and hanged himself from a rafter by winding his cravat round his neck twice. His brother, getting up and finding Martin's shirt across his bed, went down to the privy and found him stark naked. He cut him down, covered his privates with his coat and tried to hide the fact that he had committed suicide by 'reporting that he had died at his business.' However, when the surgeon arrived and opened up his head, believing him to have died of an abscess, he saw by his neck that he had hanged himself. The following day the coroner held an inquest and the jury was about to give a verdict that he had hanged himself while asleep but this was doubtful as he had been reading an account of men half-hanging themselves as an experiment. Roseenstan was buried about ten or eleven at night the following day in St Mary Magdalen's parish churchyard, nobody being present except the bearers and the parish clerk.

Between ten and eleven in the morning of 23 October 1681, Mr William Cardinal hanged himself from the door of his bedchamber. He was found by his maid after twelve o'clock, wearing only his shirt and his nightcap and there he hung until that evening when the coroner and jury viewed him. They declared him of unsound mind and about eleven that night he was buried, stark naked. He had had a troubled conscience for cheating his college for three or four pounds when he was bursar the previous year and got in trouble with the warden. He sunk into melancholia and the previous summer had thrown himself into the water in Magdalen Water Walks but did not manage to kill himself.

On 26 August 1688, Thomas Ashwell, a Merton scholarship-holder and tailor's son, hanged himself in his chamber after dinner, 'being in want and love', and hung there till the stink of his body betrayed him.

He was taken down and buried, towards the upper end of the Grove about three next morning.

From16 July 1782: a man named Haddon who had been sentenced to death for mail robbery was found dead in the condemned cell in the castle. He had fastened himself to the bars on the window by using his sheets. The inquest gave the verdict '*Felo de se*'. Haddon was buried in the Botley turnpike road the next day but friends dug up his corpse shortly afterwards and covered it with lime in order that it should not be taken away for dissection.

From 14 October 1848: Stephen Judd, a turnkey at the city gaol, told an inquest that 52-year-old William Cook who had hanged himself there, had arrived after being committed for trial at the sessions for a felony apparently well and showed no signs of mental health problems. Judd searched him and then put him in a cell where he took his clothes off to have them examined, the usual procedure on entering the gaol. He then left Cook, telling him to put his clothes back on. After about ten minutes the warder returned and found the prisoner hanging from the bars at the window of the cell. He cut him down immediately and the prison governor sent for Mr Symonds the surgeon who came with his assistant straight away; however the prisoner was stone dead. The jury returned a verdict of '*Felo de se*' and the coroner issued a warrant for Cook to be buried between the hours of nine and midnight that same night.

From 13 February 1865: 'a very single-minded suicide' managed to hang himself. Coal dealer and agent for Ellis and Sons of Leicester, George Burdett aged 49 had previously attempted to do this from a beam in his stable in Jericho but his servant found him almost straight away, untied the rope and got him down. He stayed long enough to make sure that Burdett went back into his house then hurried off to the White Hart Inn in Cornmarket where a traveller from Ellis's was staying before a meeting with Mr Burdett. He told him what his master had tried to do. In the meantime, however, Burdett had recovered his rope and gone next door to St Sepulchre's Cemetery where he hanged himself on a willow tree. He was found soon afterwards but by that time it was too late to save him. At the inquest the coroner heard that Burdett had money troubles which was the reason that the meeting with the Ellis's representative had been disturbing his mind. The verdict was 'death due to temporary insanity'.

From 2 December 1876: 'A painful sensation was created on Wednesday evening upon its becoming known that a son of Mr. Carter, cabinet-maker 48, High Street, had committed suicide by hanging himself in the back premises of the establishment.' The young man was 22 years old and said to have been in low spirits for some time because he was out of work. He had quarrelled with his mother about half an hour before he was found hanging from a hook over a doorway stone dead.

The jury at the inquest had viewed the body which was by then lying on a bed in a barely furnished loft where the young man and his brother usually slept. Members of the Carter family testified that the deceased had also been on bad terms with his sister who had refused to talk to him for ten months because he had used obscene language when talking to her. They heard that he was kept short of money and also that he had hoped to take his young woman to a ball at Christmas but he did not know how he would be able to do so. The room was cleared while the jury reached their verdict which, unanimously, was 'Felo de se', despite the fact that they had done their best to arrive at a different one. The jury members donated their fees to the Radcliffe Infirmary and the body was ordered to be buried at eight o'clock that evening in Holywell Cemetery, without religious rites.

From 16 May 1891: Elizabeth Solloway aged 40, the wife of butcher John Solloway of York Place, St Clement's, strangled herself in the garret at the top of their house. Her husband stated that she had been in very bad health for some time previously with a heart disease and had been 'very queer' at times. Four years ago, when they were living at Cowley she had tried to hang herself. Her father had died in Littlemore asylum just over a year ago, and she had been fretting about this and in fact had often raved about it and said that a carriage and a policeman would come for her.

At Sunday dinner the week before, she had announced that she was going to do away with herself and asked that her children should be taken care of. When her husband begged her to calm down, she replied that she had been to Iffley intending to do away with herself, but had been prevented from doing so.

By the Thursday she seemed better but when John left for work about seven-thirty it was the last time that he saw her alive. When he returned for dinner, he asked where she was and was told by their daughter that she had been around recently. A search revealed her in the garret, lying on the floor, quite dead and black in the face but still warm. He noticed some string in her hand and round her neck. It had been wound round five times but not knotted. The inquest heard that Mrs Solloway's sister had died some five months ago in Wales and that the family 'were all very excitable'.

The coroner wished to look at the string but a policeman who had been called had taken it away. The coroner's officer stated that the deceased had already very nearly succeeded in killing herself in the same way twelve years before and would have done so had John not been there to prevent her. The jury returned a verdict of 'Suicide whilst in a state of unsound mind'.

Throwing oneself into deep water must have been tempting in a watery city such as Oxford and if a suitable place was chosen there was no going back. On 20 August 1692 Elizabeth Simons, servant maid to a bed-maker at Wadham College drowned herself at Patten's [later Parson's] Pleasure in the University Parks. She was pregnant by an unnamed Master of Arts and commoner of Wadham who had returned to his birthplace of Plymouth where he was born. The girl's body was examined and the pregnancy discovered. It was the reason why her employer had turned her out of his house and not knowing what to do, she drowned herself.

From 3 March 1786: 60-year-old Mary Parker was found drowned early one morning in a stream near the stables behind Christ Church. She had stabbed herself before throwing herself into the water. The verdict was 'Lunacy'.

From 13 April 1878: a startling rumour had circulated round the city to the effect that Mrs Weaving, the wife of a surgeon of Queen Street, had been discovered in a water tank at the back of the house. Sadly, this proved to be true. Mrs Weaving had been depressed since a boating accident which had taken place almost three years previously and resulted in a relapsing fever. Her condition had worsened and she had shown suicidal tendencies by throwing herself into water as a sort of fixation. Her family and friends had taken what they hoped were adequate precautions. Unfortunately, however, she had aroused no suspicions at all in the hours leading up to her death.

On viewing the water tank the jury at her inquest was at a loss to understand how Mrs Weaving could have crammed herself into it as it was only just over ten inches in width with the bar of the ballcock dividing it in two. She must have clambered onto an upturned barrel and then forced her head under this bar and once in, escape would have been impossible. A bruise on her face showed this. By curious and horrible coincidence, Mr Weaving had just heard that his wife's father had taken his own life by an overdose of laudanum, but she was unaware of this at the time of her death.

The jury was certain that Mrs Weaving had not been in her right mind and gave the verdict that she had been found dead from suffocation in a tank. Fees were donated to the Radcliffe Infirmary.

From 11 September 1886: the Hollybush Inn at Osney was the scene of an inquest on Emily Ellen Talboys, aged 24, the wife of David Talboys, a college servant of Marlborough Road, Grandpont. Her body had been found in Hinksey Stream, with some of her clothes hanging from a nearby bridge, but it was impossible to say if it were a case of accidental drowning, 'whether she was there without any explanation,' as the coroner put it, 'or whether she did it herself intentionally from being not quite right in her mind.' What did seem certain, though, was that she had not been pushed.

Mr Talboys stated that they had been married for about six years and that his wife had had a baby some two months ago. He had brought to court a letter written by Emily while he had been away from home saying that Mr Hitchings, the surgeon whom she had consulted, considered that a small quantity of drink would affect her head. He had returned home straight away.

The girl's mother-in-law stated that shortly after six the previous Wednesday morning, the deceased had visited her house, knocked three times, and slipped a note under the door. Mrs Talboys managed to call her and bring her back to the house and sat her in a chair. The note read: 'Go down at once. Do a good part for my darling baby. Drink has been my end. Emily.' Mrs Talboys did not think that she had been drunk at the time of the visit. After a few minutes, however, she jumped up, ran off and was not seen again.

Shadrack Harris, a labourer from Ferry Hinksey, said that he had noticed something in the water near the path into Oxford. He thought it was human and continued into the city to inform the police. This was about quarter to two in the afternoon. Then he returned and saw the body recovered. The policeman involved, PC Scaldwell, stated that near the bridge over Hinksey Stream he saw a woman's jacket, a hat, a necktie and an umbrella on the bridge. On looking at the body, he noticed that the back part of the head was clear of the water and the rest immersed. In the corpse's pocket was a partly written letter in the same handwriting as the one slipped under Mrs Talboys's door. It read, 'Dear Husband, — Never any more will you see me, unless it is in my grave; I have been mad with drink, for — .' There was then a scratch, as if the ink had run out. An envelope addressed to her husband in Windermere was rolled up with the letter and with it in the pocket was a halfpenny. The jury decided that 'the deceased drowned herself while in a state of unsound mind.'

From 9 May 1891: Margaret Ann Cleaver of Worcester Terrace, the daughter of Alfred Thomas Cleaver, a compositor in a newspaper office, was 24 when she committed suicide. Harsh words had been exchanged between Margaret and her father concerning money. Mr Cleaver stated that he had tried to push her out of the room but strongly denied having hit her. He said that 'it was time they parted' meaning that she should find a job. He then left the house and on his return found his daughter apparently reflecting on what had been said. They went to bed about ten-thirty without exchanging a word. When he came downstairs the following morning, Cleaver found a piece of paper lying on a table. On it was written in pencil, 'Good-bye all, you will find me above Godstow,' so her father and brother went there and after a brief search found her body in the river, just as she had written. A single set of footprints was found in the mud leading down to the water.

One of the jury commented that, as she had a comfortable home and everything that she needed, something very harsh must have been said to drive her to such a drastic action. Another added that people's temperaments are different and they will react accordingly. The third pointed out that as there had been plenty of time overnight for Margaret's temper to cool down, something exceptional must have happened during the row with her father. The jury returned the verdict: 'That the deceased committed suicide, but that she was not in her right mind at the time she committed the act.'

From 3 October 1891: a mysterious case of drowning came before the coroner at the Settling Room in Gloucester Green. The subject was William Whiteford Turnbull aged 22, a non-collegiate student from Kelso, who had been lodging in Walton Well Road. He had been studying for responsions, the preliminary examinations for an Oxford degree which were due in a few days. He had been to lectures and taken his meals as usual, although his landlady had noticed 'a strangeness in his manner'.

He had left home between eight and nine that evening but had not returned; on the following morning a letter was found on the desk in his room. It was signed by him and clearly showed that the young man 'was labouring under hallucination, probably caused by over-study.' His walking stick was discovered on the riverbank at Godstow Lock and a search later revealed his body in the lock. It was removed to the mortuary at Gloucester Green that evening.

The body showed no signs of violence and his watch was still on his person. No boat was in the vicinity to indicate an accident. However, it was very wrong to jump to the conclusion that he had killed himself as there was no evidence of this. The boy's father, a doctor of medicine said that he had last seen his son towards the end of August or beginning of September but had no reason to suppose that he would commit suicide.

The letter found on the desk was produced, written in pencil in a straggling way and taking up two sides of paper. In places it was barely legible but was thought to read:

> My dear Father,
> I have overheard certain things and you well know none of them are true in the least. I think they come from a Mrs [a name looking like Hass], who disliked me.
> You can thoroughly believe my last words as I die.
> Your son, W.W. Turnbull. With love.

Dr Turnbull contested the words 'as I die', although he could not positively identify the writing as being that of his son and had not heard from or about him until the telegraph saying that he was missing and from letters from his landlady and a fellow student.

The jury returned the verdict that the deceased was 'Found drowned at Godstow Lock, in the River Thames, in the parish of Binsey but as to how he came to be in the river, no evidence doth appear.'

Suicide by shooting was messy and very unpleasant for those who had to deal with the aftermath. On 2 December 1826 *Jackson's* wrote:

'It is our painful duty this week to announce the death of a Gentleman of the University, under circumstances most distressing to his family and connexions.' Henry Abbott of St Alban Hall 'put a period to his existence by shooting himself through the head in his rooms.' A pistol shot had rung out about three one afternoon and was heard by a servant working in the hall but nobody took any notice. When there was no sign of Mr Abbott the following morning someone went to call him but found his door locked from the inside. Someone fetched a ladder and climbed in through the window. It was a very unpleasant shock to find him lying on the bed with a discharged pistol in his hand. He must have put the muzzle in his mouth as the ball was found lodged in the back of his head. At the inquest, the jury heard that the deceased had been a very steady young man who had recently passed the First Public Examination for his degree; they returned a verdict of 'Insanity'.

From 10 April 1875: 'A painful sensation prevailed in Oxford on Wednesday morning last when it became known that one more name had been added to the list of unfortunate persons who have lately come to an untimely end by their own hands.' This person was architect, 24-year-old Edwin Hill of 35 High Street, youngest son of painter George Hill. He had shot himself in his father's house. The inquest heard how the body was a shocking sight. It lay partly undressed on the bed with a rifle to the breast, the trigger fastened to a rail of the bedstead by a tie. Just below the heart was a hole where the bullet had entered the body and the shirt was burnt for some distance round the wound while the flesh was blackened and scorched by gunpowder. The bullet did not seem to have gone through the body and no blood flowed from the wound.

The first witness, his older brother, stated that he had seen the deceased the previous evening looking 'fearfully pale' and realized that he 'he had taken too much to drink.' He added that he knew of no reason for his brother's action apart from the fact that 'he might have had *delirium tremens* through excessive drinking.'

It was heard that the previous day the deceased had written a postcard to a boy at the office at 113 St Aldates, where he worked, saying 'Shall not be at the office this morning; don't feel quite well. E. HILL.' Dr Tuckwell stated that 'he had attended the deceased for rheumatic fever and valvular disease of the heart, the latter of which would produce fits of despondency and mental depression and habits of intoxication would aggravate the results.' The verdict was 'Temporary insanity'.

From 18 November 1876: that afternoon, Thomas Wyndham, Fellow and tutor in Natural Sciences at Merton College, shot himself. He had given a lecture a few hours previously and the suicide was only discovered about five o'clock when his bed-maker came to his room and found his body on the floor with a gun beside it. Although a very proficient academic, Wyndham had become almost obsessed with his work and was seen in some quarters as an eccentric. He had given the impression of being quite depressed the previous week and one of the two letters found near his body was read out at the inquest. It was addressed to his medical advisor and read, 'Dear Dr Acland, I must be put into a lunatic asylum. Please put me in'. The second letter, which was addressed to his former fiancée, was not produced at the inquest. The jury's verdict was 'that the deceased had destroyed himself while in a state of unsound mind.'

On 7 July 1845 the newspaper *Sporting Post* ran this report:

> '[An] extraordinary suicide at Oxford. Between eleven and twelve o'clock, Mr Sheard, one of the most respected traders in the High Street, Oxford, threw himself from the top of his house and on the pavement. He was immediately carried into the house and almost instantly attended by a medical man but life was extinct. His skull was found to be fractured above the ear and his neck broken. A coroner's inquest was shortly after summoned and from the evidence of several witnesses it appeared that the deceased had shown decided proofs of insanity for several days but had that morning appeared so much recovered that it was not thought necessary to watch him so strictly. The deceased was greatly respected by all who knew him. He was a member of the Town Council, had served the office of sheriff and was treasurer to a charitable institution. He has left a widow and six children.'

From 25 March 1899: 'a startling and singular discovery' was made at a house in the Iffley Road, the home of Miss Helen Bickford, a dress-maker, who lived there alone because she had been unable to attract lodgers. David Wylie, her next door neighbour became aware of 'a most offensive smell emanating from Miss Bickford's home' and alerted the police who broke into the house. 'A sickening odour pervaded the place' and the officers were almost overpowered by gas fumes. When the curtains were opened the remains of Miss Bickford were discovered wearing her nightdress and lying on a sofa bed, covered by an eiderdown and a blanket. The bed was only inches away from a large, fiercely burning gas stove.

'The heat was intense and the atmosphere so foetid that until the windows and doors had been opened for some time it was impossible to pursue the investigation. The body presented a dark brown appearance, and seemed to have been tanned by the heat.' It was strange that the bedding and her clothing had not been set alight by the stove. On a table was an open Bible in which several texts from the Psalms had been marked with a cross. Several letters were found with names and addresses written on them together with instructions that they be forwarded. From the unopened mail, it was clear that she had been lying there for a week and that the gas fire had been burning all that time. The body was removed to the mortuary, prior to an inquest.

Among the exhibits was a letter addressed to Miss Bickford's brother in which she reproached him for not having visited her and for pleading poverty as the reason that he had not done so. He had not seen her for years, whereas she thought visiting every two months was reasonable. He, however, complained that his sister did not write to him, although she claimed to have done so. She had found it embarrassing to admit to neighbours that he never came.

She ended by emphasizing that she 'is not to be buried. You have stayed away through life and the hideous mockery of following me to the grave must be prevented.' She insisted that her body be offered to a hospital 'in return for which I require to be dissected and examined as to my having lived a pure life, such confirmation to be forwarded to you and to Dr G. Batten, M.D., Lordship-lane, Forest Hill. When I was ill from the tumour, do you remember? – life and people looked so different to me, death had no shadow. I felt so very glad to go, so restful, all seemed Peace; then they told me I should live. I have never ceased grieving, never seemed in touch with the world since.' She then told him that he shall have nothing belonging to her as everything was to be sold apart from the dictionary, which she was leaving to his sons. There was to be no ceremony of any kind, 'they are but idle words when acts have failed during life, and it is in the power of many round me to act, but they will not.' She ended, 'With love, Nellie.'

After discussing the possibility of suffocation and having heard all the evidence, the jury was told to decide whether to return a verdict of suicide or an open one of 'Found dead'. They decided that the deceased committed suicide whilst temporarily insane.

Chapter 14

Burials

In *Wadham College Gazette,* of January 2013, concerning the recent discovery of an unexplained skeleton on the college site, Dr Allan Chapman wrote:

> 'And what happened when you died "in residence", be you an undergraduate, a don, or a monk? Why, they gave you a Christian burial within the precincts of your domus, or house or college. In Wadham, we buried our dead either in the ante-chapel, or in the "cloister garden", between the College Chapel and the kitchens. Now without wishing to be grizzly, or give people nightmares, we have to realise that Oxford would have been a giant graveyard. And all these centuries of dead people are still with us, just a few feet beneath our floors and pavements. Not just the remains of monks, undergraduates, and dons, but also of townsfolk who shared Oxford – sometimes in a state of violent tension – with them.'

The thirty-seven skeletons uncovered in the ditch of a previously-unknown Neolithic henge at St John's College in 2008 were mostly those of men aged between 16 and 25, of sturdy build and taller than average. Each one had been repeatedly stabbed before death. From the scarring on their bones some may have been professional soldiers and some bones had been charred before burial. Chemical analysis of the bones showed that their diet had been higher than was usual in Oxfordshire. The latest suggestion is that they were a group of marauding Vikings who had fallen foul of the Saxon population and paid the price.

Although not on the same scale, there had been previous unexpected discoveries. For example in April 1821, when some men were digging

141

for gravel in the grounds of the nursery near the observatory belonging to Mr Tagg, they came across a complete human skeleton about four feet below the surface. It was about five feet long and of slight build. The bones appeared to be sound until exposed to the air and the touch of the numerous visitors who came to see them. It was impossible to get any idea about how long the body had been there because the soil was very gravelly. Brass rings resembling key-rings were found near the bones but there was no trace of a coffin and it was assumed that the person had been murdered and buried secretly.

From 15 March 1823: as a group of men were digging for gravel at Hoarston Farm, later called Somers Town, in St Giles, they found a skeleton about two feet below the surface. It had greatly deteriorated and was lying on a bed of gravel. There was no sign of any clothing but under the head was found a copper farthing dating from the reign of Charles I and by its side two brass gilt buttons and a bodkin; this gave the impression that the skeleton was that of a soldier. The items found were handed to a glazier in Broad Street called Bradford 'for the inspection of the antiquary'.

In 2012 a dedication stone plaque was erected on the path known as Deadman's Walk, leading into the Botanic Garden from the High Street in Oxford. The thirteenth-century burial ground of the Jews is now beneath a rose garden belonging to Magdalen College near the Danby Gate of the Botanic Garden. There has been ongoing speculation as to the origin of the name Deadman's Walk. Some have suggested that it commemorates the execution by firing squad in 1645 of a Colonel Francis Windebank for failing to defend Bletchingdon House against a parliamentary force. In fact it marks the route that Jewish funerals took from the Jewry to their burial ground to avoid going through the town.

Jews had settled in Britain soon after the Norman invasion of 1066 and there was an earlier Jewish cemetery sited on the opposite side of the High Street. They enjoyed the monarch's protection but were also his chattels, so that anything they owned in fact belonged to the Crown. The Jewry itself grew up near the monastery of St Frideswide in and around today's St Aldates and in the parishes of St Edward's, St Martin's and St Aldate's. However, until 1177 all Jews had to be taken to London to be buried in a national Jewish cemetery outside Cripplegate. It would have been difficult enough for the residents of the Oxford Jewry to manage this but so much worse for those living even further afield.

In 1177 Henry II finally permitted Jews to set up cemeteries throughout the country and so the Oxford community looked for a site outside the city walls as their religion would not permit them to be interred within a Christian settlement. By the 1190s the burial ground, generally referred to as the Jews' Garden, which is now part of the main Magdalen site was in use. Around the same time, however, the Hospital of St John the Baptist acquired it as part of a larger transaction and for the next forty years the two operated side by side. Then the hospital almoner asked the young Henry III for the site and was given it so that the Jews' Garden had to be given up and a new cemetery found. There is no evidence as to whether the bodies from the old site were moved across the main road to the new one.

Proof of the burial route is found in an incident of 1186 when a young Jewish man named *Deus eum crescat* ('may God increase him'), got into trouble with the town elders for ridiculing a procession in honour of St Frideswide, Oxford's patron saint. He committed suicide the same evening in his father's house. When his body had only just begun its journey to London, a wheel of the cart on which it was carried hit a hole just as it was passing St Frideswide. The corpse was tossed onto the road and its neck broken, a fitting punishment for ridiculing the saint.

After 1290 when all the Jews in the country were ordered to convert to Christianity or be expelled, the Hospital of St John claimed the second burial ground which it acquired in 1294. The fact that Magdalen College was later built on the site of the hospital explains why it owns both burial sites to this day.

When the Botanic Garden was set out in 1621 as the Oxford Physic Garden, the foundations for its walls disturbed the old cemetery and 'many Bones of each Sex and of all and divers ages were found by digging here.'

Despite having lived almost on the premises, in death Katherine Martyr was not destined to rest in peace. The wife of Peter Martyr, protestant canon of Christ Church, she died in 1552 and was buried in the cathedral. With the Catholic Mary Tudor on the throne, in 1554 Cardinal Pole sent orders to Dean Marshall that she be exhumed and her remains thrown onto a dung heap. She is believed to have remained there until the accession of Queen Elizabeth and the restoration of Protestantism. Katherine's remains were retrieved from the dung heap and in 1562 given an honourable reburial with the bones of St Frideswide, the city and university's patron saint. The resting place of both ladies is marked by an inscription on a flagstone near the saint's shrine which had been destroyed when St Frideswide's Priory was suppressed in 1538 and the pieces thrown down a well. These were rediscovered and the shrine rebuilt in the 1891 with a second reconstruction in 2002.

On 15 October 1686, 30-year-old Jacob Allestrey Master of Arts and student of Christ Church, died in the house of a nurse, Mrs Gadbury a sawyer's wife who lived in Fisher-row in St Thomas's parish. He was buried the next day about eight o'clock at night in that parish church carried by four poor men, with no cloth covering the hearse. He had stayed for seven weeks at Mrs Gadbury's house suffering from the French pox or syphilis which eventually killed him.

On 16 June 1691 Wood was invited to see the opening of the vault in Trinity College by Bartholomew Peesley, the master mason. At ten that morning the door was opened and dust shovelled away from the steps. Wood went in with Peesley and found under the north wall the body of a woman. On her right were two men's bodies, six feet long, the coffins rotten and with no inscription on them. The woman was Lady Elizabeth, the widow of Sir Thomas Pope, the college's founder.

From 12 April 1787: the corpse of a pauper, Mary Llewellin that had been buried the previous day in the workhouse graveyard was exhumed with a coroner's warrant. This was done in response to complaints that were circulating that she had been poisoned. The verdict at the inquest was, however, 'Natural death'.

During the cholera outbreak of 1832 the use of tobacco and brandy was widespread in the county gaol, at funerals and similar stressful situations as preventatives against disease. Both were issued free from parish funds for those involved in the laying out, transporting and burying of victims of cholera and other infectious diseases.

Pauper funerals could be a considerable drain on the finances of the poorer parishes. Typical costs of cholera funerals such as the fifteen that were charged to the parish of St Ebbe in 1832 were charged at five shillings and sixpence each. This included the linen for a shroud at seven-pence.

The funeral of William Cantwell of St Peter le Bailey, although not a cholera victim, provides a good example of the total cost of a funeral: nine and sixpence to the officiating clergyman, a shilling to the parish clerk, a shilling for the passing bell, three shillings for the grave, a shilling for cords and boards and another shilling for turfing the grave. From St Thomas's expenses are five shillings for brandy for ten cholera funerals, one and sixpence to a carpenter for a black coffin and from St Aldate's, funerals charged at five shillings and sixpence and seven shillings and sixpence with two shillings for burying a still-born child.

An unexpected expense was incurred when two cholera victims were taken punting at a cost of three shillings and sixpence. A letter from the beadle of the United Oxford Parishes states that the corpses of Robert Stone and Sarah Cheeseman were taken down the canal from the workhouse as far as the turnpike bridge on the Botley Road, and from there down Kite Street to the rear of St Thomas's church to avoid unruly crowds who might turn out to protest. Rumours had been circulating that bodies of paupers might be sent off to the School of Anatomy or even that vulnerable people were being killed off or allowed to die so that their corpses might be used.

Arguably the most distressing unsanitary nuisance and one over which the general public had no control whatsoever, was the overstocked urban graveyards. On 21 September 1832 the Rev W.R. Browell, Fellow of Pembroke College wrote complaining about the crowded state of St Aldate's churchyard adjacent to the college [Ms Top Oxon c269, ff192-5]. Apparently whenever a grave was opened several coffins were exposed to view. A clergyman who was officiating at a funeral 'was witness to an indecent exposure of this kind which was very distressing.' Even the pathway through the churchyard had been dug up to provide more burial space and had the unpleasant habit of caving in under the passer-by when a coffin lid gave way under him. The sexton was obliged to probe the ground with a long iron rod before attempting to start to dig, 'with a violence and disrespect to the remains of the dead revolting to our sense of propriety.'

Browell stresses that this is by no means the only graveyard in this state. Those of St Ebbe, with more than 3,000 residents, and of St Peter le Bailey, St Michael, All Saints, St Mary Magdalen and in particular St Martin Carfax being disgraceful and their clergy all at a loss to know how to improve matters. He closes with the hope that Oxford will soon get its much-need cemetery. Unfortunately, as a clergyman he was very much in the minority, and this wish was not to be fulfilled for a considerable time.

In 1974, Dr Chapman worked as a volunteer on the recently deconsecrated All Saints church that was being converted into Lincoln

College Library. There may have been as many as five churches on the site and, as he says, 'And Lord, how many hundreds of skeletons were found on that one small site alone!' Owing to the powdery dryness of the soil, excavating was done with dustpans and brushes 'to reveal skeletons packed like sardines in a tin, shoulder to shoulder, face to back of the head, to a depth of about fifteen feet, extending from folks buried in the days of King Alfred the Great to those interred in the reign of Queen Victoria!'

One of those disinterred, dating from about AD 1400 was given the popular medieval name 'Alizon' because they felt that they had got to know her so well. She had died when about 18 or 19; her leg bones were slightly bowed, possibly from rickets due to a Vitamin D deficiency. From her pelvis, it appeared that she had born a child. Dr Chapman describes 'an appallingly-degraded upper molar, surrounded by an upper maxilla jawbone perforated with a profusion of tiny holes so as to resemble a pepper pot, suggested a cause of death. A bad tooth had probably led to infection, then untreatable septicaemia or gangrene had developed in the jawbone, from which poor Alizon died after the infection became generalised around her body and her immune system gave way.'

In January 2004 the news broke that between sixty and seventy skeletons had been discovered in a mass grave on the castle site. Many of them dated from the Elizabethan period and may be connected with the so-called curse uttered by Roland Jenks in 1577. They came to light during archaeological work carried out by Oxford Archaeology prior to the development of the area the previous year. A test pit revealed eight skeletons followed by more extensive work that yielded a further fifty-nine more or less complete specimens plus various additional bones that have been dated from the mid-sixteenth to the mid-eighteenth centuries. Most of the skeletons were young men but there were five women in their late 40s. Several of them bore signs of dissection and three had the tops of the skulls expertly removed and in one case the skull had been separated from the body.

It seems almost certain that these were those of criminals executed and used by anatomists at the school at Christ Church or the Old Ashmolean building, but this brings the number above the legal limit. Until the later eighteenth century criminals were strangled, which does not show on the skeleton, instead of having their necks broken. Some skeletons had their hands clenched and in two of their fists a button and fragment of cloth were found.

In Oxford there were three places where executions were carried out, Oxford Castle, Green Ditch and Gownsmen's Gallows which was reserved for members of the university. The last public execution took place at the castle in 1863, but hangings continued within the prison walls until the middle of the last century. In 1546, Henry VIII created the Regius Professorship of Medicine at Oxford and soon afterwards undergraduates reading medicine were required to study for six years during which period they had to be present for at least two dissections before taking their degree. Before they were allowed to practise, they were obliged to perform a minimum of two dissections themselves, an innovation which meant that for the first time English medics were forced to both see and perform dissections on human subjects.

In 1624, Richard Tomlins founded and endowed a lectureship in Anatomy at the university, attached to the Regius Professorship and the first lecturer received an annual salary of twenty-five pounds out of which he paid three pounds to the surgeon who assisted him and two for the collection and eventual 'decent buriall, of the body and all the necessaries thereunto'. Lectures were held in the Anatomy School in the Old Schools Quadrangle before migrating to the Old Ashmolean Museum in 1683.

The success of the teaching and study of human anatomy led to its own problems in obtaining enough cadavers. After the Lent Assizes, the reader was expected to get hold of 'a Sounde body of one of the Executed persons,' if at all possible. This was not practical during the summer months or during Michaelmas Term when no Assizes were held. The source of corpses was increased by a charter of 1636 permitting the reader to demand the body of any criminal executed within a twenty-one-mile radius of the university.

The will of Matthew Lee stipulated that about £2,300 should provide a building where the study of anatomy could be carried out, together with a readership and the costs incurred in obtaining corpses. The Anatomy School, designed by Henry Keene in 1766-7, was erected south of Christ Church Hall. The anatomy lecture room occupied part of the ground and first floors of the building and dissections took place in the basement. This 'had a receptacle in which the bodies are deposited after the lecture was completed. This place is a hole dug in the ground to the depth of about 13 or 14 feet; and to remove all offensive smell. A little stream is turned through.' Corpses were brought into the school, nicknamed

'Skeleton Corner', through the back entrance of Christ Church, 'without scandal to the college'.

To supplement the insufficient number of corpses legally available for dissection, body-snatching took place throughout the country. Fresh corpses fetched a good price at anatomy schools despite the fact that anyone caught stealing a corpse might himself end up on the gallows. The theft of a corpse was not a crime as it was not considered property although items such as shrouds were and that is how many thieves were convicted. In addition, the public reaction to anyone known to have interfered with a dead body would have made his life unbearable.

Jackson's gives an account of a thwarted attempt at grave-robbing: 'This week a set of Abandoned Miscreants were discovered in an attempt to rob a grave in Magdalen parish Churchyard in this City, in which the bodies of a woman and Infant had been interred two nights before. They were alarmed just as they were going to break the ground, upon which they took to their Heels and the bodies were next day taken up and re-interred in the Church to prevent any future attempt.' It also reports on criminals' corpses being legally taken off to the Anatomy School after being hanged.

On 24 May 2002, the Bishop of Oxford, the Right Reverend Richard Harries held a service in the gaol's cemetery. The *Oxford Mail* quotes Claire Sandford, the instigator of the idea, as saying, 'When I was taken on a tour of the prison site I was struck by the distressed feeling of the place. We all talk about these issues, but this made it seem so very real.' Some thirty criminals executed at the prison lie there in unmarked graves. The bishop's blessing took place almost half a century after the death of the last man to be hanged at Oxford Castle.

However, not every corpse that ended up on the dissection table was that of an executed criminal. One was Samuel Mashbourne, the Wadham undergraduate who was killed by a bolt of lightning on 10 May 1666, while boating with friends on the river. 'Prior to burial, he was dissected and his skull "opened" by Sir Christopher Wren's friend, Dr Thomas Willis, the eminent Christ Church anatomist. Because the top of poor Mashbourne's skull was sawn off to give Willis access to his brain – as specifically mentioned in the report to the Royal Society – his remains, if ever accidentally uncovered during building work, will be instantly identifiable.' Dr Allan Chapman, 'The Scholar, the Thunderbolt, and the Anatomist', *Wadham College Gazette* (1993), pp. 59-62.

On 6 June 1838 the idea of a cemetery was first suggested in the city council, and a committee was formed at once to explore the idea. In 1843 the committee reported that every churchyard in the city was full, and that some, notably St Ebbe's, were offensive to passers-by. Clerical opposition prevented the acquisition of a general cemetery, but in 1848 new parish burial grounds were consecrated in Osney, Holywell and Jericho (known as St Sepulchre's). Orders in Council in 1855 instructed that burials, except in existing vaults or walled graves, should be discontinued in all the historic parish churchyards, and in the graveyards of the Roman Catholic, Baptist, Wesleyan and Congregational chapels, the workhouse, the Radcliffe Infirmary, and the castle gaol. In the three new parish burial grounds and Summertown churchyard, burials were to be made only in plots already reserved, and in accordance with regulations for new burial grounds.

On 1 January 1844 Cox wrote:

'The question of a public cemetery – that is, a burying-place open to all persons, of all creeds, or even of no creed was discussed at a general meeting; when eight of the parochial clergy, who wished for the Church to bury its own dead, left the room, on finding that their views and wishes were not favourably received by the meeting, who were for a general cemetery. For effecting this, however, nothing was done then or since; whereas the Church view soon began to show its truth and reality, by the successful efforts made for the acquirement and arrangement of the three parochial burial-places. These were soon consecrated, with their respective chapels, &c.; but where is the cemetery? There is something very pleasing and charitable in the idea, that all who call themselves Christians should have one common dormitorium or resting-place, where they should lie down together, at peace in death, though separated in their lifetime, and awaiting their common resurrection; but in the working it out (as to officiating ministers, the rites and forms to be used, &c., &c.) difficulties and collisions would necessarily arise. In Oxford the purchase of the burial-grounds by a subscription was soon effected, indeed the site for one of them (Holy Cross) was given by Merton College; they were to be for all persons, on the same footing as churchyards had been, and for the use respectively of the adjoining parishes to which they were allotted.'

On 17 February 1849 *Jackson's* carried a long letter to the editor:

Sir, - The first interment from the parish of St Martin's in that part of Holywell Cemetery which was appointed to us by the Burial Committee took place last Sunday.

Every one is aware that the rivers adjoining this City are now lower than for several months past, and that this ground is considerably above the level of the river at all times, but I am informed that water was found on first opening the grave at two feet four inches, and that it speedily rose to within ten inches of the surface. The consternation of the sexton may well be imagined; he abandoned the grave, and dug another on a higher spot; as shallow as was at all consistent with decency, but the bottom was covered with water when I saw it. The funeral was attended by a large congregation, and I will leave you to judge of the feelings of the parties present when they looked upon the coffin after it was lowered to its resting place.

This, Sir, is to be our latter end, and because a majority of the parochial Clergy of this city (some eight or nine gentlemen) chose to oppose themselves to the general feeling of the University and City, which was in favour of a General Cemetery in the dry ground of St Giles's Field, we, the parishioners of St Martin's are to be deposited in a sponge, and there converted into aedipocire [a fatty, wax-like substance formed on animal corpses as they decompose]. This is the doom pronounced upon us by the Burial Grounds Committee. Here they have brought, and here they have left us, and we are, at our own expense, to attempt the, I fear, hopeless task of draining this sponge, or raising the ground at the rate of some 6000 cart loads per acre, for less will not do it. I leave this matter for the consideration of my fellow parishioners and the University and City at large, merely adding as I think it right I should do, that our worthy Rector, having always repudiated the allotment, which he considers was illegally made to us, refused to sanction the interment, and took no part in the ceremony.

I remain, Sir, your obedient servant,
St Martin's, Feb.12, 1849   A CHURCHMAN

From 28 July 1849: a funeral at St Thomas's attracted a great deal of interest due to the unusual form that it took. Despite the pouring rain, there was a much larger crowd than is usual at such occasions. It seems that Fanny Bossom, a 16-year-old girl 'of exemplary character', the daughter of Mrs Bossom, laundress, of Fisher Row, died of consumption and her funeral was arranged by the vicar. This gentleman was present when the body was being laid out and 'had the arms of the deceased laid across the breast, and a cross in nails placed at the head and foot of the coffin.' The funeral was to take place at nine-thirty in the morning and around that time the funeral procession left Fisher Row. When it reached the church it was joined by local school children who walked ahead of the corpse, scattering flowers along the way while choristers and singing men chanted the burial service. On entering the church, three clergymen assisted in the ceremony and the choir chanted various parts of the service, as they did at the graveside. When it had finished the mourners and many other people went back into the building and took communion. A collection was made at the service and contributions were as large as the poor parishioners were able to afford.

From 7 November 1856:

> 'A remarkable funeral took place (viz. that of a young chorister of Magdalen College choir, named Bird) at the burying-ground of St Cross. The boys of the school, about forty in number, followed the hearse to the cemetery, where they were met by a surpliced choir of thirty. The Burial Service was sung with great feeling and thrilling effect. N.B. The monument soon after raised to the poor boy's memory upon a scale rather large and grand for its little occupant provoked the following expression:

> 'On approaching the large tomb of a little boy.
> I saw the tomb and cried, with deep surprise,

"Surely some great one 'neath that structure lies."
I read, and found a little "Bird" at rest,
A bird too humble for so large a nest.'

St Cross is the alternative name for Holywell church and cemetery that had been found so sub-standard in 1849.

In 1876 the cemetery committee of the Local Board reported that it was not possible to comply with the orders of 1855. St Thomas's and St Clement's churchyards were sometimes still used and although the three parochial burial grounds were expected to last for a further nine years, conditions in Osney and St Sepulchre's were bad. Many rate-payers, supported by the Medical Officer of Health, requested the setting up of a general cemetery, and the Local Board instituted a Burial Board the same year. On 9 June 1888 a proposed site was discussed for a general cemetery at Rose Hill, on land belonging to Christ Church. However, this dragged on until the following year as a price could not be agreed. Finally eleven acres were purchased at Rose Hill and a further thirteen acres from the Dean and Chapter of Westminster Abbey also in 1889 and eight more acres in 1890 from the Earl of Abingdon.

On 2 November 1878, *Jackson's* carried an account of the funeral of Sarah, wife of the Regius Professor of Medicine, Sir Henry Acland, in Holywell Cemetery. After a detailed description of the cortege, the mourners and the ceremony itself, including the coffin 'of polished oak, with brass furniture', the account concludes:

'Many of those present carried sprigs of myrtle and flowers, and many beautiful wreaths were placed upon the coffin, which was deposited in a brick vault in the northwest corner of the Cemetery. The funeral, which was conducted by Messrs. Elliston and Cavell, was most simple and unostentatious, thus fitly harmonising with the life and character of the estimable lady whose remains were laid to rest. There were no plumes on the hearse and no hat-bands were worn. Most of the blinds were drawn and shutters closed of the houses on the line of route, and similar tributes were paid by many in other parts of the city.'

The *Morning Post* of 24 January 1898 carried this account of the funeral of Dean Henry Liddell:

FUNERAL OF DEAN LIDDELL

'The body of the late Dean Liddell was on Friday evening brought from his residence, Ascot Wood House, to Oxford and placed in the Latin Chapel of the Cathedral. On Saturday afternoon the funeral took pace in the graveyard adjoining the south side of the cathedral choir. Shortly before the time fixed for the Service, the body was taken into the central aisle, the coffin being completely hidden with beautiful wreaths, the Prince of Wales sending one composed of arum lilies, camellias, white roses and lilies of the valley, attached to which was a card in the Prince's handwriting: "For auld lang syne, from an old Christ Church friend, - ALBERT EDWARD." The Cathedral was filled to overflowing. Her majesty the Queen was represented by Colonel Sir Henry Byng, the Prince of Wales by Major-General Sir Stanley Clarke, and the Duchess of Albany by Colonel Waller, R.E. Representing the University was the Vice-Chancellor (the Rev. Dr Magrath, Provost of Queen's College), while the Reading Extension College was represented by Mr W Palmer.

'Among others present were the MPs Lords Curzon and Valentia and Col, Morrell, Lord Abingdon, and the Heads of Houses of All Souls, Merton, University, Balliol, Lincoln, Exeter, Pembroke, Corpus, Brasenose, Jesus, Oriel, Trinity, Keble, Magdalen, Hertford, Worcester, St Edmund Hall, St Mary Hall, Mansfield. Also present were the various University officials, from the Proctors to the Controller of Lodging Houses. A special saloon was attached to the 1.20 train at Reading to bring the chief mourners, principally members of the Liddell family.

'The fully choral service was conducted jointly by the Bishop of Oxford and the Dean of Christ Church. The grave which had been lined with moss studded with white flowers had been prepared next to that of Dean Liddell's daughter, Edith, who had died in 1876.

'The inscription on the coffin read: "Henry George Liddell, Dean of Christ Church, 1855-1891. Born 6 February, 1811; died 18 January 1898."'

What the article does not say is that Dean Liddell was the father of the more famous Alice Liddell, the inspiration behind *Alice in Wonderland*. Mr and Mrs Hargreaves, Alice and her husband were listed among the mourners. By strange coincidence, the announcement of Dean Liddell's death in the *Aberdeen Weekly Journal*, was immediately followed by an account of the funeral of 'the Rev Charles Lutridge [*sic*] Dodgson (Lewis Carroll)', at Guildford, who, says the paper, was 'of an unpretentious character'.

Acknowledgements

Jean Butler for her help with the illustrations
Dr Allan Chapman, Wadham College
Judith Curthoys, archivist, Christ Church
The Governing Body, Christ Church

Index